MAKING ART
IN THE MIDDLE OF
MADNESS

A Guide for Waking Up from Your Fear-Trance So You Can Create Like the World Needs You To . . . Because It Does

HOLLY SHAW

Praise for this Book

"*Holly Shaw delivers a vital reminder and re-envisioning. It's a brutal wake-up call from a strangely nurturing drill sergeant. Humbly, honestly, and at times hilariously she navigates that murky and mercurial world of artistry through troubled times. Her sirens' song is a clarion signal for us to rise up for the sake of the world as well as for our own prosperity, as we know deep-down we must. Create art to combat crisis: It's a beautiful, witty and relevant message for us right now.*"

- Dan Cantrell,
Emmy award winning composer,
accordion wizard and grower of high quality beards

"*Being creative and making art can be challenging in normal times. The pandemic has complicated it further. If you're feeling stuck or lost in this time, this book is the perfect guide for jolting you back into your creative, aligned self. With deep thoughts about the fear trance and the Three Fears Of Devolution, coupled with real-life exercises and tips for using your fear to fuel you to make something different, artists, writers, performers, and creatives of all kinds will find this guide useful and inspiring. Holly's voice is clear and smart. She has a gift of making things that seem complicated or "woo woo" feel grounded and accessible. This guide will change your life if you let it.*"

- Amy Estes,
Comedian, Humorist, Writer (Huffington Post)

"*Her playful storytelling illustrates why it's more important than ever to create right now and how to overcome the internal forces that tempt you with giving up—to 'take fear and turn it into light.' As a stand-up comedian who still gets pricked by nerves before every performance, I'm going to be carrying her Love and Fear Elixirs with me when I go on stage—even if that stage is a computer screen!*"

- Jennifer Mason
Stand-Up Comedian, Licensed Acupuncturist
and producer of the Sofa King Funny Show

"*With both elegance and casual frankness, Holly takes the reader-artist by the hand and shows us how to use our usual human cocktail of responses to what scares us -- fight, flight + freeze -- to nourish our art-making, rather than shunt it. She generously draws on her extensive experience onstage and her coaching work with artists-across-all-genres to not only point us to potential pitfalls as we create, but to guide us with clear steps to become conscious agents of change. Brava Holly!*"

- Kellita Maloof,
Conscious Burlesque Mentor and Author of
How To Create A Burlesque Solo ... From The Inside Out

Also By Holly Shaw

The Creative Formula:
Compose, Choreograph and Capture Your Masterpiece

Making Art In The Middle of Madness:
A Guide for Waking Up from Your Fear-Trance So You Can Create Like the World Needs You To . . . Because It Does

For permission requests, please contact: holly@performersandcreatorslab.com

ISBN - 978-1-7362024-0-1

Written by Holly Shaw
Content editing by Keith Gordon
Manuscript editing by David Horwich
Author photo by In Her Image Photography
Cover Art and Interior Book Design by Heidi Sutherlin

Published in the United States by:

Performers & Creators Lab

Oakland, California

www.performersandcreatorslab.com

Printed in the United States of America

*This book is dedicated to our shadow selves:
the Outlaw, the Rebel, and the Fabulist who lurk inside,
waiting for their chance to kick ass, throw wild parties, and make
things just a little bit more fun along the way with their chaos.*

Table of Contents

Foreword

When Holly asked me to pre-read this book, I said yes with tail-wagging enthusiasm without even knowing the subject matter. From the moment we met at a Digital Hollywood conference a few years ago, I felt like I had found one of my people. Throughout the years we've found different ways to work together and after reading this book, that initial spark was reaffirmed.

There has never been a time in my life when all at once every person, company, organization, institution, industry, tradition, plan, dream, routine and rulebook were consumed by a tidal wave of uncertainty. Until 2020. The world found itself in the middle of uncharted water all in the same boat without life vests, leaders or light houses. COVID-19, both pandemic and pawn, has changed the course of history and life as we know it forever.

For twenty plus years I've been in entertainment PR and brand marketing, working with musicians -- from indies to icons -- and suddenly I felt unqualified to give advice or help navigate brands and careers that I had meticulously cultivated and protected. There were too many holes that needed filling so whatever educated conclusions I could come up with would be based on shifting sand. Then personally, as a children's book author and artist, I had to question whether I would even be able to continue doing what was so fulfilling and joyful.

Let me just say this, the universe is rarely subtle, so if we miss something, we are not focused on living life the way we want to be. At a time when I felt unsure of how to move forward, Holly's book showed up in my inbox. After reading the last words of the book, in a stream of consciousness, I shot off this email to Holly:

> *Everything I need to know, as a creative professional today, swimming with millions of others in a sea of pandemic, financial, political, environmental, social, and industry uncertainty, I just learned in your game-changing, tool-de-force 'Making Art in the Middle of Madness'*
>
> *Do you feel like you have been leading up to this??? I do. I am really really proud of you . . . and the title ROCKS, btw!*
>
> *RR*

If you haven't looked, the number of cookie-cutter, broad-strokes, passive "pandemic self-help books" being marketed right now is only rivaled by the number of hand sanitizer options available. We don't need generic answers or hypotheses about "the new normal" or "life after COVID." We need real solutions and tools that work from people who understand us, speak our language and have as much at stake in the game as we do. Holly is one of these people.

Holly is a creative arts multi-threat (dancer, actress, choreographer, comedienne), coach and hypnotherapist who has spent the past several years looking at the role fear plays in preventing creative professionals from reaching their potential. Over her impressive career, she has developed tools and techniques for actors, singers, dancers who are struggling with stage fright, change, uncertainty or calling it quits. *Making Art in the Middle of Madness* is what her career has been building up to and from the first story she shares about handling crisis from 30,000 feet, Holly's authenticity, understanding of humanity and well-earned battle scars keep you engaged, and make you feel empowered and wanting to learn more.

You understand as much as I always have that she has your back and she's there to help you succeed. I have struggled to figure out what to call this...a book? A game-plan? A philosophy? Survival guide? Tool box? Secret weapon? Soul caffeine? It is all these things.

Holly shares the lessons she has learned in the trenches and the tools she has developed to navigate the psychological, emotional, social and even physical realities and roadblocks of being successful at what we all were put on this earth to do: Create. In the context of the world today, the guidance, tips and exercises she shares are crucial game-changers. She does so with an accessible, authentic, insightful authority that makes you realize we don't need a cheerleader on our side right now; we need someone who understands our position, has the training tools we need to be our best selves, knows what it takes to be successful, has our backs and wants to win as badly as we do. The book you are holding in your hands right now comes from such a person.

Roger that, Universe.

Ron Roecker,

Award-winning author and illustrator who moonlights as an award-winning brand marketing and entertainment PR strategist for global brands, celebrities, and artists.

Calm Person on the Airplane

I'm not always good in a crisis. Oh, well, maybe in heat of the moment I am. There are times when I can be unbelievably calm and helpful even as everything spins out of control ... It's the moments just after the crisis where I start to fall apart.

Case in point, airplanes. I'd always been pretty good on them until one day several years ago, on a flight from Reno to Oakland, we encountered some turbulence. The plane shook at first, taking us by surprise as it lurched to one side. Then an eerie silence and stillness. The passengers held their breath, and then—a drop. It felt like we suddenly dropped fifty feet or more. Then bumps and more drops.

Whenever I encounter turbulence, my eyes dart to the windows. If I can just see the sky or get some orientation of where we are, then I feel better. But this time, there was no relief to be found through the windows: just a thick dense fog that I couldn't even see three inches into. I could feel myself getting queasy, and I noticed the anxiety start to rise.

The passengers began to react. Gasps. Screams. Someone wailing, "Oooooohhh no!!!" And all I could think was, "Shut up everyone! You're freaking me out!" I began to breathe. Deep breaths. And then I went into complete and total denial. "We're going to be fine!" I said to no one in particular. "This isn't that bad."

A lady across the aisle turned to me with a scared look on her face and asked, "Really? Do you fly a lot?"

"Oh yeah," I lied easily. "I mean, airplanes are built for this kind of thing. Right now, we are being tossed about in the air and it doesn't feel great, but we're not gonna fall out of the sky or anything. We're good."

She seemed to breathe in what I was saying and I saw a flicker of relief.

We held each other's gaze. I made myself smile with my eyes. I'm an actor. I figured it out.

Eventually, a few other people around us noticed our calm little bubble and I turned to them too.

"Yikes!" I said with mock terror, then repeated with my best reassuring mom voice, "We'll get through it. Planes are made for this."

"Whoooo! Wheeee!" I said with false enthusiasm, like a bored teenager riding a rollercoaster. The man next to me, his eyebrows furrowed in distress, kind of cry-chuckled.

Eventually, some of the people around me started to follow along, turning their "oh nos!" into "whooooos!" I finally even elicited a couple of timid "wheeees!" followed by some more cry-chuckling.

Then the plane started to even out and fly with just the usual bumpiness. If you closed your eyes, you could imagine you were on an old-timey wagon bumping along a dirt road. I closed my eyes and breathed. Most of the passengers had quieted down, though at the front of the plane I could hear someone crying faintly, and someone else comforting them.

The chaotic part of the flight was over. The passengers slowly hunkered down once again, timidly turning towards their *In Flight* crossword puzzles and earbuds.

And then, that's when I broke down.

All of a sudden, the anxiety I had been pushing down came roaring back, and I twisted my face into a bunch as I tried to silence the sobs. My face became a wet faucet—my head was hot and I pressed my hands over my heart, trying to calm and comfort myself.

I continued like this until the plane touched down, and then I clapped and cheered like a big crying mess. I didn't give a crap about the people staring at me in a mix of embarrassment and bewildered disgust.

So you see, great in a crisis, total crying mess afterwards. I guess you could call me a "Delayed' Panicker."

The power of being calm in the face of chaos and madness is described perfectly by Buddhist monk and author, Thich Nhat Hahn, in his book *Being Peace*:

> "In Vietnam, there are many people, called boat people, who leave the country in small boats. Often the boats are caught in rough seas or storms, the people may panic, and boats can sink. But if even one person aboard can remain calm, lucid, knowing what to do and what not to do, he or she can help the boat survive. His or her expression - face, voice - communicates clarity and calmness, and people have trust in that person. They will listen to what he or she says. One such person can save the lives of many."

Call me what you want to afterwards, but in the moment of chaos, I can often be the calm person on the boat—or on the airplane, in this case. And if it hadn't been me that day, then it would have been someone else. Whenever there is a problem, you'll often find at least one person who feels "called" to rush in and keep things orderly. At our best, that is what humans do for each other.

But what if the airplane never lands?

What if the airplane just continues to shake and heave? For days, weeks, months?

What does that calm person on the airplane do when the crisis seemingly never ends?

This is where you have to draw on something greater than just "faking calm" and being the hero in the moment. This is where you have to steer into the fears, use that adrenaline to push you to greater heights, and learn to work with others.

And this is where this book begins.

What I Mean By "Madness"

The turbulent airplane hasn't landed.

As I'm writing this book, just weeks from the presidential election of the year 2020, we are several months into a pandemic that isn't going away anytime soon. We are faced every day with the realities of harsh injustices, a great divide among the populace, corrupt leaders, and impending environmental doom. And I know that I'm putting this pretty mildly.

The "madness" of which I speak are these external factors in the world that push our "fight, flight, or freeze" buttons. Those occurrences, whether political or environmental, that make it hard to get up in the morning and leave us with a sense of doom and gloom and questioning the point of doing anything at all let alone making art. I'm talking about the madness that hopelessness thrives on.

Having our world upended by a contagious virus, thrown into uncertainty by a threatened democracy, and on a very personal level, having our lives go from a sense of free mobility to now having restrictions on where we can go, how many people can be there and how we're allowed to interact once we're there elevates any fears or anxieties that may have already existed inside of us.

All of these external factors which I'm calling "madness" can make it feel very difficult to mobilize ourselves to make art -- and especially to display that art in the public eye.

That's why I decided that it was time to share what I know about fear and particularly in regards to how fear lives inside the performing artist: how it works on the nervous system when you're on stage, how that translates to what we're experiencing in the world now, and most importantly, how that can actually help us.

In this book, I'll dive deeply into the systems that are most likely running you: The Three Fears of Devolution (normal responses to your extraordinary circumstances), and your shadow selves (those archetypal parts of you that are good at hiding and can at times help and hinder you). We'll shine a light into these dark places and I'll show you how to navigate your way out.

This is the time for us to really understand fear. Not only understand it, but also learn how to wield the powerful energy it can give us access to: like those seemingly superhuman abilities to achieve calm on the turbulent airplane. As timely as this manuscript may be, I have to imagine these lessons will never be extinct. I don't see us achieving some kind of happy go lucky utopia any time soon and so, even if you're picking up this book and the year is 2068 (Wait! You're still here on planet Earth? Can you still even breathe that air?) the guidance and introspection offered by the following pages will still prove useful.

Who This Book Is For

This book is for performing artists: actors, comedians, musicians, dancers, storytellers – those of us who tend to display our art on our person and do it on stages, in film, and in television. Nevertheless, all types of artists or creatives, including writers, sculptors, painters etc., are bound to find value in the guidance here in this book, because all artists have to overcome fear in order to bare tender offerings to the world. . . and a world in turmoil even more so. Even those who may not call themselves "performers" or "artists" but who find themselves in the public eye, like social media influencers, speakers, public figures, will also find these lessons valuable. For they too have to get into the limelight and figure out a way to do it without flinching.

Anyone who tasks themselves with creating, speaking up, or being seen in the world will want to read this book. If this is you, then on some level, you may have a sneaking suspicion that now is not the time for you to shrink under the bed covers and give up on your creativity. This is your time to be creative, to spark the solutions in the minds of others, because if not you – the one whose job is creativity and expression – then who else is ready to do it?

In this book, I will often use the words "perform" and "create" interchangeably. This is because even the writers, painters, sculptors of the world have to bring themselves to perform – even if it is alone, in a studio, in the service of showing up to make their work. And the reverse is true: I don't know any performers that aren't on some level constantly creating – even if it is in the creative interpretation of someone else's words, as in the work of an actor – and I have already said I'm addressing here the performing artist because their art doesn't exist without their body, their emotions, their mind and so it is even more imperative that they master control over their fear as it affects all parts of them: their body, their emotions and their mind.

You may have already guessed it, but you there reading this, you are the calm person on the airplane.

Or at least, that is who I hope that you become through doing the work of reading and working through the sections in this book. I'll guide you through the systems that are running you, namely fear, and show you how you can not only manage that fear, but also learn to use it as fuel to create with.

It is your calling right now to be the calm . . . and to not only spring into action in the moment and then fall apart afterwards, but to find a way to make your calm long-lasting and sustainable.

But Why Is Art Important? And Why Now?

I know in times of distress, art might feel frivolous to you. It feels almost like an act of rebellion or of self-indulgence. You find yourself questioning how it fits into survival of our planet and harmony between people living on it. But to question its importance is to misunderstand what it is that an artist does when they focus on creating something: It takes 100% of their attention in the moment to do it and do it well. You can't stand confidently and convincingly on a stage when your whole body is trembling. You can't expand on a melody when you're consumed with terror. Performing forces a resolution of fear in the very act of doing it. It gives that energy of fear a place to go and changes the substance of it in the process. Not only that, but that shift is transmitted to anyone watching the performer. The audience, the witness, the crowd feels it to and is changed by it.

Also, the majority of what we consider to be the creative process is actually a form of problem solving. New artistic pieces, ideas, and offerings are not born out of thin air. They are a resolving or reimagining of what already exists. And so therefore, making art necessitates being in a solution-oriented mindset in order to do it.

When an artist is able to bring themselves to making or solving rather than the problems of the current moment, then a shift takes place not only in their mind but in the mood surrounding them. It can feel almost as though the very molecules of the air subtly change to encompass more possibility, more hope, and more promise.

The making of art in the middle of the madness is life-affirming AF! It's pushing against your instinct to shrink, to hunker down, to protect, and to merely survive. It bucks the limiting trajectory of this shrinking and instead makes space for the same care and attention given to creating something to be given to all of life-living in general. In a sense, by creating something you're saying, "Not only life matters, but how we do life matters."

The year is 2020 and the plane hasn't landed. We don't know when it's going to land. And yet we still need to get to work. To live. And to try to live well. And that means making art is imperative.

What's Wrong With You?

So you might be reading this thinking, "Yeah, that's great, Holly, but how am I supposed to get up and create when I can barely get out of bed some days? I don't feel like the calm person on the airplane, ready to burst into a show tune or even a cry-chuckle! I feel more like the person heaving into a throw-up bag in row 10."

Yeah, I get it.

It is not an easy time for anyone, and artists—who weren't exactly having a great go of it to begin with—are having an even harder time now. In short, there is nothing wrong with you—you are just grieving. You're grieving the loss of those avenues for making money and sharing your art. As I write this, the bars in California are still closed, as are the theaters, comedy clubs, dance studios, and all in-person classes. All of these are CLOSED CLOSED CLOSED! Due to the pandemic, most of our outlets as performers are all deemed dangerous places to be. And so, it would be completely natural that you might be grieving a loss.

We have no idea when this is going to be over and we can go back to "normal." In fact, normal as we knew it is starting to look like a grungy hitchhiker left behind in the rearview mirror. They seemed friendly up close, but we feel a sense of relief now that we look back at them. What we knew as "normal" wasn't necessarily the right fit after all.

Part of our "new normal" is a sudden dependence on technology. Even before the pandemic hit, streaming had decimated the income of many independent artists in the music industry, and more and more people watch content in their houses rather than go out to theaters. With everyone spending hours on social media channels and YouTube, we performers have found ourselves creating even more unpaid content with less audience just to try to "keep up."

Whereas performing in a crowded theater can come with its own set of fears, at least there is the potential to receive the warm energetic transmission that comes from live performance—hearing the applause, seeing the excited faces, feeling the connection with the audience. Now with an online audience, not only is there less connection (or in some cases, like pre-recorded videos, with no realtime connection at all), but that audience has gotten meaner. A different kind of stage fright has arisen, not of the "angry crowd" but of the YouTube trolls, Twitter rage, and public ridicule that can damage a person's livelihood and reputation in a flash.

Because of technological advances, performers have become more visible over time and perhaps sooner than they are prepared for. Nearly every type of performing artist now has an online presence. And so now you're testing your work out in full view on the internet, eliciting attention, whether good or bad, sometimes before you're ready. And the audience is meaner. Blog writer Jeff Goins, having experienced his share of internet trolls and haters, considers why people are meaner online:

> "My suspicion is it's the anonymity of the Internet that causes people to say things online that would make their mothers blush. To run their mouths in ways they'd never do in someone's home."

These attacks on the internet create a hostile environment for you when you are trying to put you and your work "out there." In a sense, you feel like you were born to be seen, even though all you want to do sometimes is hide.

On top of being afraid of the criticism, you may also be worn out by the relentless anonymity – by the hard work it takes to even be heard among the many who are trying to get their work into the world. Artists used to have the fear of being good enough. The path to get to the top was unclear and dominated by the elite, but if you were actually good enough, then there was the potential to really "make it" and have your work affect the world. But now, with so many ways to produce, share, stream, and disperse content, the fear isn't only about being good enough—it's also about not being found. There is a despair that can set in from realizing that even if you are good enough, you still may never be heard.

And so, this is what is wrong with you: You're afraid of being seen and also of not being seen enough! You're questioning if it's worth it to work so hard to be better if better doesn't make a difference in the end.

Do you feel like I "see" you yet?

Have I adequately let you know that I understand your pain? That I totally get why you don't feel like making art and instead just want to watch that funny video about the cute grouchy dog and work on perfecting your margaritas?

I get it. This time sucks for you.

And yet, in so many ways, if you have always felt called to be a performer, you have been preparing for this all along.

Yes, you read that correctly.

And on top of the push to the online world that as an artist you've experienced over the last ten to twenty years, you are finding out that not only do you miss your in-person audiences, you might actually fear your online ones.

You feel like you were born to be seen, even though all you want to do sometimes is hide.

Let's be real. A performing artist—whether you were trained in the traditional sense or you sprang up through luck, grit, and good timing as the social media star—never gets 100% immune to the fears: of being criticized or of not being good enough. But maybe, just maybe, because of your wily coyote creativity, your ability to connect and bare your soul, and your imagination that's poppin' with new ideas. . . maybe you're made for these times. I believe that you are.

Throughout these pages, I'm going to show you how awesomely prepared you are for this madness we're living in as a performer. I will show you how you can use the same muscles and skills you've developed in this brutal career of yours. And by the time we're done, you are going see that you are...

The Calm Person On the Airplane That Hasn't Landed Yet.

"I do not fear the soldiers, for my road is made open to me."

\- Joan of Arc

No, I'm Not Going to Make You Wear Pants

It's not your job to make your inner rebel wear pants in front of the computer. It's your job to guide them into action.

This is how we're NOT doing this book.

I'm not here to push you to wake up every morning and brush your teeth, pretend like everything is normal, put on street shoes to sit at your desk because that's what some expert on the internet told you would help you feel more work-oriented and productive.

No, I'm not going to make you wear pants.

That is an outside-in bullshit approach.

Ok, so wear pants if you like it and it makes you feel better, but let's get real and address things at a deeper level. Let's not make a mockery of your fear and pretend everything can be solved by, well, pants.

When you're in the middle of madness, to pretend that nothing is going on, and that we're all supposed to be normal and productive when the shit hits the fan is absolutely NOT a long-term solution. It's not a time to bury our heads in the sand or sigh and wish "everything would go back to normal." Because I'm here to tell you, it isn't. It never is.

I'll tell you what—that kind of boot-strapping, grit-your-teeth-and-bear-it kind of mentality doesn't serve you, but it is what you've been told to do for a very long time. It has lulled you into a kind of trance because sustaining the status quo, even when it's ridiculous to do so, is exactly what other people hope you will do.

Is your inner rebel kicking in yet? Good! Let them out of the cage.

Now is the time to let them gnash their teeth and snarl. Your inner rebel, along with your other shadow selves, has been waiting. Hungry. Intensely pissed at injustices and ready to seek revenge. Ready to turn that anger into action.

It's not your job to make your inner rebel wear pants in front of the computer.

It's your job to guide them into action.

And in this book, you'll learn just how to do that . . . without ripping everyone to shreds. Hopefully.

The Fear You Know:
Stage Fright

Before we look at any other fears that you might be dealing with, we are going to begin by looking at a fear you almost definitely already know on some level: stage fright.

Even if you are one of the few artists who hasn't experienced this on the stage, it's likely you've encountered it somewhere else: the nervous tummy the night before a big test, the pressure on the basketball court to hit the free throw, the jitters before the big meeting. Everyone experiences performance anxiety at some point in their life.

Laurence Olivier, Barbara Streisand, Megan Fox, Adele—can you guess what all of these artists have in common?

They've all experienced crippling stage fright.

In a recent study conducted by Gordon Goodman at the Fielding Graduate University in Santa Barbara, he found that more than 80% of professional actors have suffered from stage fright at some point or another during their career.

He also found that, contrary to popular belief, stage fright has nothing to do with age, lack of experience, or talent. It can afflict you when you are just starting out or it can seize you for the first time in the middle of your career.

Your Role: Center of Attention

Whenever you step out onto a stage or in front of a camera, you're assuming the role of center of attention. It is presumed that all eyes will be on you, so you have the responsibility to do something with all that attention. Will you excite the audience? Transport them into another world? Or will you make them feel awkward? Or make them fall asleep? (Yikes!)

Being on stage isn't for everybody. Many people—in fact, most of the world—actively avoid being in front of an audience. Research has found that public speaking is people's greatest fear, even greater than the fear of death! So, if you love being in front of people, then go ahead and give yourself a pat on the back! You are doing something that few people are willing to do!

Being in front of people and commanding their attention can be daunting. If you choose to do it, then you understand the responsibility to deliver something wonderful. It's a lot of pressure! I want to acknowledge you for taking on that role. It's instant leadership.

That responsibility to deliver is exactly what can make it so challenging and heartbreaking when you drop the ball. Because you know that carrying the energy is your job.

When the world around you is experiencing madness, you might feel as though you're carrying the weight of the world on your shoulders. You are used to delivering the goods on stage, and so when faced with conflict and issues offstage, you might experience an acute sense of stage fright. Just as when you're performing you feel highly attuned to the audience and what's going on around you, so too you feel highly sensitive to the needs of the greater world around you. It's always been your job to usher the audience through the story and make everything play out well on stage and so it's hard to drop that tendency even when you're no longer playing that role. This is how the pressure of the current madness in the world can feel exactly like stage fright.

Not to brag, but these days I have a pretty good relationship with my stage fright. I welcome the heightened sensation of it, and I have learned to lean into the force of the wave. When I flub up or something disastrous happens at a show, my immediate response is most often, "Yes!" because I'm experiencing a moment of aliveness.

As a comedian, I once had an entire audience literally yell "Booo!" at me and urge the host to get me off the stage. You'd think that would be a traumatic memory, but in truth, it's one of my favorites. In that moment I remember feeling that, even though they didn't like me, at least they were paying attention, and in that attention there was possibility. I felt an adrenaline rush in that moment and was able to use it to finish out that particular set with great laughs from the audience. I even received hugs from some of the audience members on my way out of the venue. I had figured out a way to get them back on my side again, and just as a couple can feel closer after a fight, everyone in the room that night felt closer after that encounter. Ever since then, I've relished these kinds of opportunities to get my hands dirty and see what I can do to turn things around.

But I don't want you to think it was always this easy...

The Young Actress Choking In Auditions

The honest picture of my life journey as a performing artist is far more nuanced than that. Sometimes it is muddied with fear, trepidation and boring mediocrity.

From as far back as I can remember, I was bitten by the performing bug. I needled my parents to put me into dance and theater, and when I was older, I nagged my dad relentlessly until he took me on a trip to Chicago to get my own acting agent. All the while, I occasionally had ecstatic and wonderfully charged performances, but I had lots and lots of horrible, limp, and terrifyingly awkward performances as well. I was a mixed bag. I was the bi-polar bear of performing. Hot one minute and cold the next. It was truly confusing . . . but exhilarating enough to make me want to continue.

In 2016, I published a book, *The Creative Formula*, which became an Amazon bestseller. Over the years I had helped hundreds of artists (some of them Emmy and Grammy-nominated artists) overcome their stage fright and creative blocks, but with the book, I realized that I was now helping thousands of artists all over the world—something that I could have never imagined as a young actor auditioning for Burger King commercials in Chicago twenty-five years ago. . .

When I was just a teenager, I lived in Indianapolis, but my agent was in Chicago. This meant I had to travel back and forth from Indianapolis to Chicago every time I was up for a part. My family didn't have a lot of money, so my dad and I took the Amtrak train. It was a five-hour trip one way and another five hours back . . . which is a very long time to sit and stew about how your audition went.

I'll never forget an audition I had for a commercial. I was fifteen years old. I went in, said the few lines, and the director said, "Do it again. Differently this time." I remember being so nervous that my hands were shaking and my heart was pounding. So, I did it again—exactly the same as before. For some strange reason, I wasn't able to change a thing. I felt like a puppet of myself with the strings not attached. The director sighed and said, "Again please. Differently this time." I watched myself in horror as again, I did the exact same read.

Deep sigh.

"Thank you very much," he said dismissively, and so I was out the door and back on the train for my five-hour trip back home to Indiana.

I wish I could tell you that this was the only time this happened. But truth be told, it happened nearly a hundred times, for nearly every audition from age four-teen to sixteen, resulting in nearly a hundred miserable five-hour return trips on the Amtrak from Chicago. Sometimes I muddled through, sometimes I did just ok. I was very lucky that I had one or two casting directors that kept calling me back. Many of them didn't.

I'll never forget the day that my dad sat me down after what was maybe the ninetieth audition. I remember the way he looked in his white work shirt that was yellowing at the armpits. He was already nearing sixty years old at this point, and I remember how his long, elegant hands, hands I inherited, trembled ever so slightly as he asked me, "Are you sure you want to keep doing this?"

We were on the train coming back from Chicago, and as he said this his hands folded together and shook from the bumpy train. I understood why he asked. The stakes were high. My parents had very little extra money and these trips were cost-ly: I missed school, and I was auditioning poorly. I never told him how bad it was in the room, but I knew my highly intuitive dad could tell from my mood afterwards.

But the most obvious sign was that I wasn't landing any jobs. The whole situation was really disheartening.

But something inside of me was reluctant to quit. I felt a swell of emotion at the thought of stopping now, and the words just fell out of my mouth, "I want to keep doing this!"

I knew that I was supposed to be doing this. I had this feeling that I was born to be seen! And I knew that I needed to keep going.

What I Did to Turn It Around:

My first acting coach was from Steppenwolf Theatre. The producers hired her to help me when I landed the starring role in their ABC Afterschool Special called Love Hurts. Do you remember ABC Afterschool Specials? They were short TV films geared for teens, tackling issues like pregnancy, drugs, relationships. Well, Love Hurts was about my character, Christie, dealing with an abusive boyfriend.

I worked with my acting coach during pre-production, and not only did she help me craft the character, but she got me out of my self-consciousness. She taught me acting techniques for taking up space and for using that nervous tension to create crackling energy in a scene. It was only the beginning, but I began to fall in love with the craft of acting. I had gotten my first taste for what was possible with my own little vessel of firecracker expressiveness mixed with the emotional hormonal charge of your average teenage girl.

"If you have stage fright, it never goes away. But then I wonder: is the key to that magical performance because of the fear?"

– Stevie Nicks

Since then, my interest in stage fright and performance energy has grown. I noticed interesting things about my fear. As I began to work more and perform more, I found myself having these really transcendent, almost spiritual experiences onstage and in front of the camera. My stage fright got worse, but in contrast, those occasional transcendent performances started to blow the roof off. And so, I began to study the relationship between the energy that captivates and the energy that can tear you apart.

I started mastering my mind and teaching the process to others. I became a hypnotherapist and began coaching hundreds of artists, actors, Grammy-nominated musicians, Emmy-award winning artists, and internationally renowned dancers overcome their stage fright and master that energy to turn it into magnetism.

I've come to learn that if you are having heart palpitations, sweating, shaky legs, nervous stomach, it doesn't mean that you shouldn't be doing this. It means that you should. It means that there is energy trying to move to you and through you— it's simply a matter of learning how to get up to speed with that energy, reframe it, and use it to your benefit.

Holly Shaw

Fear and Ecstasy: Two Sides of the Same Coin

I descend the steps on the side of the hill and watch the bodies circle around the fire, moving and playing music. There is an air of anticipation as people stand off to the sides, their hands clasped in a motionless reverence. I approach slowly, walking through the crowd and feeling the attention in the room turn to me as I become more visible. Like a wave coming at me, it sends a little tremble through my body and I stumble ever so slightly — imperceptible to anyone but me.

Looking for reassurance, I turn to the faces around me and notice the eyes of Helena dart a judging glance from my chest and then quickly back to my face, giving a thin-lipped smile. I waver briefly in my costume decision. Is this top too revealing? Perhaps it's a distraction. I feel nervousness and self-consciousness mounting. Does everyone see this? Perhaps I was too bold to raise my hand to dance for this ceremony. Who do I think I am, anyway? I feel my legs trembling and notice sweat on my upper lip. Is the fire so hot or is it just me? All of a sudden I'm very aware of my backside and feel the urge to hurl myself to the side and hide behind one of the many big fur-clad men who are doing nothing but grinning and clutching their beer steins.

The first thing I'd like to do is to unpack stage fright and talk about what it is.

This is really important, because if you don't really understand what is going on with stage fright, then you will make up all kinds of stories about why you're having it. Until you really understand it, you might make up the story that you somehow mean to self-sabotage yourself, or that you aren't good at auditioning, or that you always mess up, or that you are out of control. Or, worst of all, that you don't have what it takes to be a successful performer.

SIGNS OF STAGE FRIGHT VS. SOMNAMBULISM

Signs of Stage Fright	Signs of Somnambulism
dry mouth or over salivating, swallowing	swallowing because salivary glands are activated
sweating, "flop sweating," cold or hot hands or feet	change in body temperature, either getting hotter or colder
fuzzy eyesight or tunnel vision	eyelids may flutter from eyes rolling back into head
pounding heartbeat	heart rate may increase
trembling or shaking	trembling or shaking

Let's start first with the symptoms of stage fright.

Here's some common symptoms people experience when they're in the middle of stage fright:

Sweating, dry mouth, racing pulse, trembling hands, knees, lips and voice, nausea or feelings of uneasiness in your stomach or bowels, vision changes, or loss of words or memory of what you're supposed to be doing next.

Stage fright is a natural response to an unnatural situation. Think back to ancient cavemen and the conditions they likely faced. If there was a mob of people all looking at one guy, what do you think that guy would be thinking? These people are going to kill me, eat me, or use me for bait—right? There was no good situation where you'd have the whole tribe focused on you and this would trigger a response to flee, fight or freeze. We have since evolved from those days, but our brain chemistry still has that flight, fight or freeze function.

Being in front of people causes an adrenaline response in our bodies that is well-meaning—it's an attempt to prepare us to fight off an enemy, flee from them or freeze and make ourselves unnoticeable. The blood travels away from our brain and into our extremities, giving us extra energy in our hands, arms, and legs (and also causing us to shake or tremble). In a sense, the body is trying to hook you up to the superpower that adrenaline provides . . . it just maybe overdoes it a bit for this day

Stage fright is a natural response to an unnatural situation.

and age. When you are on stage, you don't actually need to fight or run away—you just need to remember your friggin' lines.

So that's the deal! Stage fright symptoms don't mean you are a nerd or weirdo or inexperienced—it's just your body trying to help but getting in the way.

But there is more. . .

Would you like to learn something about stage fright that no one else is talking about?

As I became a certified hypnotherapist, I learned about what it takes to induce a trance state and what a deep trance state looks like. When you go into a trance state where both the body and the mind are relaxed, this is called somnambulism. As a hypnotherapist, I was trained in the signs of somnambulism and how to recognize when someone is experiencing this deep trance state—and guess what I found?

The signs and symptoms of somnambulism, or deep trance, are startlingly similar to the symptoms of stage fright!

Here are some of the symptoms someone experiences in somnambulism: change in temperature, becoming flushed, change in pulse or heart rate, eyelid fluttering, tingling, trembling, change of breathing, the need to swallow from active salivary glands. From the outside, these don't sound like the sensations one might experience when calm, but in fact, they are what transpires in a deeply relaxed state of a person in trance and are often even pleasurable to experience.

Now, I should be clear: this doesn't mean that a somnambulent trance and the fight-or-flight response are the same thing. Science pretty much debunks the idea that stage fright (fear) and trance (ecstasy) are the same thing because they work on different parts of the body. Stage fright works with the sympathetic nervous system (which prepares the body for the "fight or flight" response) while trance appears to work with the parasympathetic nervous system (which inhibits the body from overworking and restores the body to a calm and composed state). And yet their symptoms can appear similar . . . almost as though they are two different sides to the same system.

> So, are these two seemingly opposite things—an enhanced state of fear and a deep state of relaxation—actually two different sides of the same coin? And if so, then who's to say that you can't learn to flip from one to the other as easily as tossing a coin?

Even though they're working on different parts of the nervous system, I've discovered that with the right tools, this kind of fear (that works on the nervous system) can be used to induce a trance state. And that trance state can be anything

"A subject [of deep hypnosis] may report an experience of radical alteration in the size of his whole body or a portion of it" He may say, 'My legs have stretched out so long they feel as if they are way over by the door now,' or 'My arms are like great swollen objects on the arms of the chair, probably the most common changes reported are the swelling of the head, mouth, and arms. Sometime the lips feel so swollen that the subject finds it hard to enunciate."

- Gill Brenman, Hypnosis and Related States

It can be an all-consuming trance of fear, or it can be a trance of calm that borders on ecstasy. It all depends on how you direct yourself. Your body sends you the signs (all the symptoms of stage fright or somnambulism), and it's your job to learn to interpret the signs differently. Believe it or not, this energy can be not only good, but productive.

This is where it gets really exciting.

I want you to think about an out-of-control water hose spraying every which way. That's what it can feel like when your fight-or-flight response is out of control. The fear can create not only a bodily response but also a fast downward spiral that's hard to turn around until you hit bottom. But with some training, that powerful flow can be like a controlled water hose that you can direct wherever you want it to go. As a performer, the attention is on you—you can harness that energy and direct it into a powerful experience for you and everyone in your vicinity. You take fear and you turn it into light.

I shake myself out of my own mental spiral. Where did I go? What am I doing? I chuckle. Wow, I really started to go down a weird path there. Of course I'm wanted here. This is it. I take a big, deep breath and let the fear drift away. I trust that I chose correctly, and I send love out to Helena regardless of her weird look. I send my attention into my feet, feeling the caresses from the sand warmed by the fire.

The drums are entrancing now. The group has reached a cohesive groove and I know it's only a matter of time before the flute or violin decides to begin, and that'll be my cue. I pull back my shoulders and stand tall, closing my eyes and noticing the heat on my eyelids, and wait for my body to tell me it needs to move.

Temple dancing. As I enter the circle and surrender, I find myself seeking those ways of letting my body, my voice, my whole self express itself, delight me, until I'm tingling and positively shivering all over. Tears running down my face, I'm surprised and delighted by what movement comes out of me. Then I finally just let go of the watcher, the witness, the one who can too easily begin to judge, until even this watcher leaves the room… And my spirit is moving my body and I am just in a state where no words exist. Where there is only feeling. And I become the feeling. This is where I meet myself in ecstasy. This is where I meet spirit and know beyond any doubt that I belong.

Holly Shaw

Understanding Your Love and Fear Elixir

We are here to get the recipe of your Love and Fear Elixir.

Figure out what makes you tick, and then use it, unpack it, unwind it, and harvest it so you can move forward and make great art.

You are unique. Just like every human being on the planet, there's a pile of experiences you've had throughout your life—good or bad, healing or traumatic, expanding or hindering—that make up who you are as a person and as an artist. All of these experiences inform your decisions and your path in life. I call this your Love and Fear Elixir.

I'm sure if you were to ask any person to explain "why" they do what they do, you might get a very nebulous or long-winded explanation. That's because behind all of our decisions is a messy, complicated, intoxicating elixir of love and fear: there is the love of what we do inextricably linked to our fears about doing it. We aren't necessarily born with this love and fear elixir, but it's something that develops over time:

For example, I've always loved working alone in a studio, but I like a studio with windows. I enjoy the added thrill of knowing that someone could walk by the window and see me at any time. This craving for solitude combined with potential lookie loos was probably ingrained in me as a child when I would dance at the end of my driveway while waiting for the bus to come. Cars flying by would see just a flash, an instance of my performance, and the idea of how that might delight, confuse or wow them, thrilled me and became a part of my work ethic.

As I grew into adulthood and became more self-conscious, a fear of not really being good enough arose out of this. I felt like my teachers and casting agents might see a "flash" of me but I would have a hard time sustaining the energy. The fear of never being able to measure up for an entire performance became a driving factor that was debilitating at first but eventually made me work harder until I could sustain my energy for an entire act. So, that initial imprint – dancing for cars passing by – became over time part of my Love and Fear Elixir. I was in love with the process of working while on display, but it disabled me with fear when I thought too hard about what it all meant.

The Love and Fear Elixir is often something we cling to unknowingly. We allow these imprints and initial stories to shape our identity, and while they often inform why we choose what we choose, the Love and Fear Elixir can also be dangerous when imbibed in large quantities. When we believe too steadfastly in our own misery, we miss the opportunity for change.

And yet, your unique Love and Fear Elixir often keeps you compelled (addicted) to create, to continue to uncover the experiences and shape yourself anew. Knowing your WHY is powerful. And revealing your why can help you move on if you need to, or at the very least get re-inspired. That is why in the chapters of this book, you'll be met with questions, tasks, missions should you choose to accept them! Everyone will answer them differently, but in those answers you'll find your unique recipe to your Love and Fear Elixir.

This book isn't just information. It's a guide through the systems of your soul. Through your fears, your shadow selves, and the very places where you want to curl up and hide.

Because creating art in the middle of madness isn't just about you overcoming the madness all around you—it's also about understanding your madness within.

How We're Doing This

We'll start by taking a look at the systems that have been running you so you can start recognizing them and unraveling yourself from that downward spiral that fear can create. You'll get to look deeply at each of The Three Fears of Devolution and meet your shadow selves head on—because they are here to play too. But more on those characters later . . .

Once you understand the fear, then I'll share with you how you can plug back into your power by connection: with yourself, your community, your audience, and your creative soul mates. I'll show you how you can brave the new terrain together using your creativity to meet our crazy world head on.

If you're able to do those first two things, connect and create, then you'll find yourself uniquely positioned to begin crafting your story how you want. As you re-write your story and alchemize your pain into something new, your Love and Fear Elixir starts to brew to perfection. You might be surprised to learn new things about yourself: You may not want a happily-ever-after after all, for example. You might just really dig turning the pages of your never-ending story.

Finally, I'll share with you where this all leads: your potential impact. Because your art doesn't stop living when you press "post" or leave the stage. The resounding echoes of what you create in the world are unmeasurable. Even if your audience is small, your reach may be larger than you think.

Throughout this book, in addition to new tools that you can put into practice, I'm also sharing some incantations and invocations along the way. Because this

Behind all of our decisions is a messy complicated intoxicating elixir of love and fear. We cling to it, we allow it to shape our identity and while it often directs why we choose what we choose, it can also be dangerous when drunk in large quantities.

Holly Shaw

work we're doing—kicking down the old systems and building up the new—isn't just something that happens on the logical side of our brains.

This is not a math problem.
This is soul work. And so I use soul language.

You'll find that my approach is non-academic. It's meant to be that way. It's my hope that through the irreverence, humor, and candid language that not only can you hear me better, but perhaps I can help call out a part of you that's been in hiding—the imaginative child within you that's been dying to play. Our fears love to take over our imaginations, and so it must be through the imagination that we do this work.

When fear hits the body sometimes our spirits take off. Oh, they'll answer the phone if we call but they're not sticking around for the madness. And so I've added not only practical work, but also elements of the mystical to this book in order to subtly engage your subconscious mind, conjure your most powerful self, and call your spirit back into your body. If we are going to find a way to land this plane, we need to get all parts of us helping.

This book isn't just information. It's a guide through the systems of your soul.

If we are going to find a way to land this plane, we need to get all parts of us helping.

Waking Up from the Fear Trance

There's a pandemic going on and it is worrisome, life-threatening, already devastating to families, communities, small businesses, but the thing I'm most worried about is fear.

We're being run by fear these days.

In fact, I would go so far as to say that we are so caught up in it, you could almost call it a fear trance.

Obviously, there's a reason we might have some fear. In fact, some folks feel justified! Finally! A good excuse to fear something. Our lives and livelihood are threatened after all!

But while we should be taking the hint from the fear in this instance and using it to guide our precautions, it doesn't mean we have to live in constant fear.

For example, I wake up every day and listen to the news, and when I go to the grocery store I wear a mask, and I stay six feet apart from people, but that doesn't mean I have to wake up every day in fear. Taking precautions is different than living in fear.

It's good to become aware of how much this world that we live in is forcing a fear–based mentality on us.

Think about this:

You wake up and scroll through social media. Then you may or may not spend your day on the computer. Most likely you end your day streaming something to watch online. In a sense, all of this consumption of content fills you with fear that is subconsciously running you. It is its own kind of hypnosis.

Make no mistake, the news outlets and advertisers are brilliant hypnotists! They repeat things, they show them continuously, they add a catchy jingle or dramatic sound effects, they stoke an emotion in you, and then keep riding that. So, you're being hypnotized all the time whether you're aware of it or not. But you always have a choice in hypnosis:

Do I want to go along with this or not?

As a practicing hypnotherapist, I'm here to tell you what every hypnotist knows: all hypnosis is self-hypnosis. Meaning, no one can make you be hypnotized. You always have a choice of where you're going and what you're letting in.

You always have a choice of where you're going and what you're letting in.

So where in your life are you letting fear run you?

Often, we don't even realize when we're making decisions out of fear.

A few years ago, I was dating someone and we had a weekend away planned at a mutual friend's house. The day before the departure, I got a text message from my boyfriend letting me know he had taken a job in the opposite direction of our weekend plans and was in fact already hours away. Well, it appeared he wasn't going to make it.

I was furious that he went back on his word and wasn't going to show up after we had already made plans. When we were back in town, we argued about it. He made lame excuses and then went back and made other conflicting lame excuses that didn't match up with the first ones.

Finally, after much back and forth and late-night discussions, he finally came out with the truth, "I was afraid that I would be uncomfortable there (at the place we were going). I feel like that person has a crush on you and it would have made me feel weird all weekend."

What amazed me about this was that it finally felt like the truth. And I realized he couldn't have told me that at first because I don't even think he knew that was the real reason. He made up all these other excuses for bailing, but finally, when we got down to the bottom of it, we discovered that fear was running him.

Here are a few stories I've encountered from clients about how fear was running them. You may recognize some of these yourself.

For me, fear can show up in starting new business ventures, new product ideas. I've been so successful in some areas in my life that I fear what it might look like to start over at something else. What's gonna happen if something doesn't take off the way I desire? And so that can keep me from moving forward or taking action sometimes.

I lost my job and now I'm losing my unemployment. I'm fearful for my financial future and I'm calling in a career that is creative and connective that I would actually enjoy during our current pandemic times. But I'm so afraid that it's not out there that I find myself just reaching for the lower-paying, boring jobs I've had before.

Fear is a messenger. Fear is telling us, "Hey, look over here, it's important to look at this!" But then the panic can rise up and take hold if we don't choose to receive the message and do something about it.

It sucks to be in that place of indecision.

You see, it takes a lot of energy to stay stuck. We think to ourselves, Oh, it takes so much energy to be motivated or to make a change, or to take action, or actually go and do the thing or break up with that person. But it actually takes more energy to stay stuck and do nothing!

You might not notice it if you've been stuck for a while because it gets normalized. You think, Should I or shouldn't I? I don't know. Your mind ping-pongs back and forth, and all that travel is exhausting and unsettling. Literally. Your mind isn't settled anywhere.

It's like you're grasping the sides of the riverbank and the river is trying to take you. Creativity is always flowing. Moving towards something, never staying put. So if life is trying to pull you along and you're clinging onto the banks—then it takes a lot of energy to stay there.

Your Particular Brand of Stage Fright As An Artist

Whether you're actively putting yourself in the world or not, there's a special fear that comes from being an artist. The first step is wanting people to look at your work, and the next step is finding more people who will look at your work, some of whom will pay you. And then you want even more people to look, which makes it easier to get that good-paying job, gig, or project. The ideal scenario is that you get more and more well-known—and make more and more money from your art.

Well here's the thing: eventually people are going to see you and not like you. If you're doing your job, then there will be some people that don't like it. There will be some people for whom you are a catalyst for confronting what they're uncomfortable with. You are the catalyst for their change. . . if they choose to take it. But, often times, it shows up first as discomfort, dislike, mean comments, heckling, or trolling.

Being on the receiving end of some of that is the natural progression of being a successful artist. You kind of hope you're making work that pushes that edge and makes people think, but it can also be very uncomfortable because we don't like to be disliked. No one likes the feeling of people not liking you. So what can you do?

You have to be willing.

Fear is a messenger. Fear is telling us - hey look over here, it's important to look at this. But then the panic can rise up and take hold if we don't choose to take the message, receive it and do something about it.

You don't have to be brave you just have to be willing.

There's an underlying fear of being disliked by others, of not having enough to go around, of not knowing what's going to happen next. You have been fed these fears for a very long time, and while they may be "well-founded," they are not helpful.

That is why I call them The Three Fears of Devolution—because they are keeping you from evolving.

If we want to make art in the middle of the madness, then we have to step up to it. We have to be bigger than the fear and willing to wake up from its hold on us.

So whether you're dealing with a breakup, a career change, internet trolls, or recoiling from the news of the day, you are strengthening the muscles for dealing with all the fear so you can be bigger than that fear.

You don't have to be brave, you just have to be willing. You have to be willing to feel that fear, recognize it as a signal, and go on anyway.

**You have the opportunity
to do something different with fear.**

You Already Know How to Do this

You already know how to do this.

The tools for overcoming your fear are at your disposal, and you have probably been using them your whole life. . .

You're just like Dorothy in The Wizard of Oz—you just needed to realize you had the magic in you all along.

Making art in the middle of madness is a bold move. Audacious, even. Artist, you are human after all. You are no less susceptible to fear than anyone else.

And yet an artist (even during simpler times) has always been asked to rise above these fears. Think about it: an artist has always been called to adventure into the unknown, get inside the lives of others, explore them with curiosity and consideration, and then boldly create as though there is enough space for them. Art is a powerful tonic for ignorance, prejudice, and reactionism. Fear robs us of our power. And art reminds us where we come from.

Not only that, but it is in the very act of making art that we provide an example of evolution to our audiences and witnesses. And what do we do to elicit this example?

We connect. We create. And we tell stories.

And so, dear artist, it is by this very same formula that we will overcome those fears we have around making our art.

> We connect.
> We create.
> And we
> tell stories.

In a sense, I'm telling you to get back to the basics and remember what you do. Use your own spells on yourself. Healer, heal thyself, and magician, do not forget the power of your own making.

As we explore the fears that are holding you back, we'll look at these ways you can use what you know to work with that fear: I'll show you how you will connect, create, and tell a new story. I'll show you examples of how you already know how to do this so you can realize just how prepared you really are to make art in the middle of madness.

You are powerful. Let's put it to work, for art's sake!

The Three Fears
of Devolution

Fear is glorious!

Bet you didn't see that coming, did you?

Fear, in all the multitudes of ways it expresses itself in our lives, is often seen something to overcome, to leap over, to conquer. And yet, I would argue that fear is also our greatest—if darkest—ally. Fear creates friction between our desires and their manifestation, and it can mean the difference between our action and inaction. But also . . .

Fear lets us know that we are traveling.

Imagine being in an airplane (again with the airplanes!) thousands of feet in the air. You are gliding along very, very fast to the other side of the planet, but you feel nothing. (Hopefully.) Provided there is no turbulence (ahem!), then there is no friction.

You are also traveling through your life—sometimes very slowly and other times very fast—and this creates a friction (fear) that lets you know you're changing, evolving, transforming. Although uncomfortable, inconvenient, and often blocking our way, fear is a signal letting us know that we are encountering something.

But it's up to us to learn to interpret that signal.

Our life's work is not to get to the point where we have no fear, but rather to learn to appreciate and translate the messages of the fear we encounter along our journey. Imagine this: You climb a very tall mountain and stand on the edge of a cliff with a huge drop off. Chances are you will feel some fear. Your body is likely to send you signals that this is a situation in which to be hyper-aware. Your legs may become weak, you may feel dizzy or nauseous. All of these things are your body's protective device so that you avoid falling off that cliff and dying.

But now say that you're on that same cliff, but this time you have on a harness. You are not going to fall to your death if you jump, but you are going to bounce and slide down the side of the cliff joyfully and safely. Now your body is likely to send you the same signals either way—hey, it's just doing its job! But now, because your mind knows that you are safe, you are in a position to begin translating that fear energy into something else like excitement, exhilaration, or . . . ecstasy.

We have many more opportunities and much more innate power to do this translating than we even realize. Fear is great—glorious even! We don't want to get rid of it. It's a necessary safety switch of our biological function, but it's often interpreted in all kinds of ways that send us backward and sideways in our evolution as a species. Fear unattended and misunderstood can fuel hatred, create war, and send us spinning into an unnecessary spiral of self-doubt.

But please hear this loud and clear: You have the opportunity to do something different with fear.

In the following chapters, I'm going to uncover the three basic fears of devolution. I'm using that word "de-evolution" on purpose as a reminder that these fears often keep us from evolving as our best selves and are used as control mechanisms by government, religion, and people in power.

The Three Fears of Devolution are:

> **Fear of "The Other"**
> **Fear of "Not Enough"**
> **Fear of "The Unknown"**

In a nutshell:

> **You're afraid that someone you don't know is gonna take your stuff, and then you won't have any control over what's going to happen next!**

Paradoxically, these fears of devolution are the same fears stemming from a biological function that our species has used for survival. You could make an argument that these fears have actually helped us to evolve: You see a stranger and hide from them; they might have killed you, but because of your natural distrust of something different, you survive, have kids, and pass on the fear of the other or the unknown.

These evolutionary fears have served us to a point, but now they are often reinforced needlessly and mis-used by our culture and the world in which we live—hence why they have become fears of de-evolution. We are conditioned to find evidence to support them, but ultimately these three fears have created beliefs that are not helpful when it comes to moving the world forward in a peaceful way. Nor do they help with making your art or being successful at it.

The same fears that have taken us this far are starting to turn on us. They have become rancid, poisoning the very water around us. They've lured us into a sleepy state of surrender.

"Here's to the crazy ones, the misfits, the rebels, the troublemakers, the round pegs in the square holes. . . The ones who see things differently – they're not fond of rules...You can quote them, disagree with them, glorify or vilify them, but the only thing you can't do is ignore them because they change things...they push the human race forward, and while some may see them as the crazy ones, we see genius, because the ones who are crazy enough to think that they can change the world, are the ones who do."

– Rob Siltanen

We cling to the system because it's all we know, but thankfully we have the power to wake up from this fear trance.

Most of us suffer from not one but all of the Three Fears of Devolution at some point and in varying degrees. One does not exclude another, and the way we interact or find ourselves in these fears can vary throughout our lives. You might find you couldn't care less about the unknown now only to have the fear triggered by an accident or a death in the family. Remember, these fears have a natural biological function. We are hardwired for them—but that doesn't mean they have to control us. That doesn't mean we are beholden to their dramatic in tensity or fatal outcomes.

Like I've said before, fear is energy, just like any other, but it's up to us to figure out how to wield it. Fear isn't as much as a liability as the lack of it is. Fear denotes there is an energetic charge. There is care.

Fear is something you can work with.

"Immanence is designing lives that work with the animals that we are...It's not about bypassing fraility or illness, no, it's about embracing all of that."

— Kellita, the Showgirl Shaman

Harnessing the Shadow Selves

As I walk you through each of the Three Fears of Devolution, I will also introduce you to the shadow self that is associated with that fear. Shadow selves are those parts of ourselves, often unconscious, that are hidden so deeply that when we do have the chance to see them in flashes here or there we are so ashamed or alarmed by them that we attempt to repress them back down. They are the demon babies born out of the fears and the baser, more selfish parts of ourselves. As much as you want to decry the fears and make them go away you just make them stronger in your effort. The harder you push, the harder they'll sing their siren song. And they are the songs of the shadow selves.

These shadow selves will insist they're on your side. And in some ways they are: they have their gifts. They manifest themselves in different guises. They'll lie in your defense, help you throw a tantrum when you're being mistreated, and will lead the way if you ever decide to leave the world behind and head for this hills. As a species procreating through thousands of years on this planet, we've relied on these fears and their shadow selves to keep our asses alive for a long time. They mean business, and they are not going away anytime soon.

So we'll let 'em live.

Eh, they're kinda fun at a party anyhow. But

are there healthier versions, you ask?

Like, are there versions of these shadow selves that aren't going to end the party by turning it into a cocaine-fueled fist fight in the parking lot of the 7- Eleven?

Absolutely.

Can you introduce me?

Glad you finally asked. Reader, please meet your shadow selves: the Outlaw, the Rebel, and the Fabulist. They're begging me to write about them.

Don't worry, your chaos makers will be along for the ride.

We'll give them a place at the table (and not just the kiddy table). They're like the faeries that must be invited to the christening or will otherwise wreak havoc and hand out curses.

What I'm saying is, don't worry. There's still room for your messy humanity. Is it just me or did waking up just get a lot more fun?

First, we have to understand what's been holding your attention for so long. We have to see the hand of the hypnotizer. And we'll do that by diving into the three fears of devolution and the shadow selves they give birth to. . .

Part I

Dealing with the Fear of The Other

Fear of The Other

Also Known As: Fear of criticism, losing face, loss of love, public shaming, being disliked

Mindset: Us vs. them

Shadow Self: The Outlaw

Adrenaline Response: Flight

Mode of Operation: Separation

Key for Evolution: Unity and connection

Limiting Belief: "I don't trust others to be their best selves and treat me kindly."

Manifests As: Self-consciousness, limited individuality, indecision, procrastination, anger, hatred, competitiveness, mediocrity, feelings of being an outsider

New Belief: "I trust that others are doing the best they can and will treat me kindly."

Trust In: We are all one

Connect: With the best in people

Create: Good stories about people where you assume the best

New Story: "People are all just doing their best in that moment. No one else is going to care about what I'm doing as much as myself, and therefore I will always be my own best champion. That doesn't mean that others won't root for me also."

Repeat Daily: "Others are a mirror for my own experience."

Malik is a successful actor, but after landing a good gig on a sitcom, his character is gradually being written off the show with smaller and smaller amounts of dialogue. Malik and his agent both know what is really going on. His crushing anxiety before shooting has come to the point where he vomits every time he is called to set. At first, he was able to compose himself by the time the cameras were rolling, but before long, the anxiety crept into the performances as well and he now finds himself stumbling over lines and sweating profusely during filming.

Part of this is due to the pressure from one of the star members of the cast, who makes joking jabs at him to "not fuck it up!" This is hard on him because he is already hard on himself and try as he might to not show it, he cares deeply what this big-name star thinks of him. But the worry of what others think of him started long before this gig, and long before he even became an actor.

He remembers his dad being very critical of him as a kid. His softball games, his roles in the school plays, his grades—all were viewed under his dad's watchful and critical eye. The memory of his father's face growing into a frown as he reviewed his report card was one he'd had a hard time shaking, even in adulthood. He always took with him this feeling like the audience was judging him. In the beginning, it was helpful to imagine his audience this way because it pushed him harder and made it that much sweeter when he got laughs and applause.

But the more successful Malik became, the more pressure he felt, and the fear of being criticized bloomed into a fear of becoming a public failure. Now, everywhere he looks in the media, he sees stories of stars who had risen and fallen only to be eaten up by a media circus for their decline. The fear that this creates in him is debilitating, and he is thinking of quitting the acting business altogether.

When we think of being a performer and shining our light on stage, most of us who have chosen that path think of this as a beautiful feeling. The opportunity to share ourselves. To shine. To create that magic with the audience's attention.

But sometimes there is a fear that lurks underneath that joy: What if people don't like me? Or what if I become a target of jealousy or hatred? What if the audience projects their own demons on to me? Being in the limelight means people will see you, and to be seen can be dangerous. History has shown that it hasn't always been safe to stand out from a crowd.

Not every artist necessarily wants to be famous, but I think there is an expectation, a kind of unspoken idea that if you "make it" then you will achieve some amount of notoriety. Making it means not having to hustle so hard for work. It means people hiring you without an audition and hiring you for a lot of money. That kind of success, especially in the world of the arts, can mean some amount of notoriety, some amount of fame. So, it's no surprise that artists may often have the desire (however secret) to be famous.

But how many would like to be infamous? How many would like to trade in their anonymity for being famous for something bad? Which would you rather be? Successful and an unknown? Or known by everyone forever . . . as a villain?

This is the double-edged sword of being in the limelight. It's great when they love you, but very easily things can turn against you.

We see it in the media every day. Orson Welles, Amy Winehouse, and Lindsay Lohan were all defamed by the media. As a society, we salivate over stories of when a great artist or public figure gets caught in a bar fight, gets caught driving drunk, or falls into drug addiction. When we are so captivated by the gossip of these events it reveals the uglier side of our attraction to stories. These tales may sell newspapers, but they also make an uncomfortable and hostile environment for a performer to feel like they can really put themselves out in the world and take artistic risks.

How can we truly step forward and be brave if we're afraid of the worst? If we're afraid of people making us wrong?

The answer to this question determines the level of risk we're willing to take. It determines how fearlessly we approach our work. How far we are willing to go to take a stand, and how much we're willing to call attention to it. Would you rather be people-pleasing and receive polite applause? Or would you rather stand courageously on one side or another of a topic and risk people hating you?

The fear of the other is one of the most damaging and cruel—not only to ourselves, but to the world and people around us. And yet it's understandable why we've developed it. History has taught us that we can't always trust others. War, cruelty, ethnic cleansing, colonialism, and even things as simple as heartbreak in romantic relationships has proven to us there is good reason to not trust others. And then that initial distrust is often exploited to further other people's agendas.

In its worst form, the fear of the other is used to promote bigotry and racism, to separate people and nations in order to conquer them or progress political agendas. On a spiritual level, it propagates a lie that we are separate. It disconnects us from our shared human experience. Fear of the other feeds paranoia and self-doubt and provides a breeding ground for competitiveness.

Indicators of Fear of the Other

Self-Consciousness

The fear of the other most often shows up for performers by way of self-consciousness. If you are worried of what others think of you, then you are constantly seeing yourself through their imagined lens. You are using them as an excuse for keeping your attention on yourself. When you're so consumed with your version of their reality and allowing your anxious imagination to fill in the gaps you can silo yourself off into a narrow lens of reality that only exists in your mind and miss things that fall outside of that—namely, what other people are actually up to.

Self-conscious people can come off as self-indulgent, selfish, only thinking of themselves; when in reality they are thinking of you, but only in terms of how you think of them. They observe others to the extent of identifying what their values and preferences are, and then use this bar (whether accurate or inaccurate) to constantly measure themselves against.

Self-consciousness can compound the symptoms of stage fright and make it all the more unbearable. You feel a little nervous in your stomach, or worried what people might think, and then you put your attention on it. As you worry more and more about yourself, you add momentum to the nervousness—and you also are more likely to miss events happening around you, creating fertile ground for mistakes and missteps.

Limited Individuality

People who have a strongly operating fear of the other will tend to shy away from those things that make them individual, unique, or special. When you're afraid of the masses, why would you want to stand out from them? This is especially damaging in a career like the arts where it is necessary to take risks and follow one's own inner voice that urges you to try something new.

Mediocrity

Art is meant to be made from a singular voice. Try to create from a consensus or agreement from the masses—or even just with all the voices in your own head, all of the "shoulds" and "what if so-and-so doesn't like it?"—and you end up with something muddied and unclear. A mish-mash of perspectives that doesn't stand for or say anything in particular. The result of caring too much what others will think is mediocrity. If you are too fearful to lean in all the way, you aim for people-pleasing work and polite applause instead of the risk-taking work that people either love or hate.

Indecision and Procrastination

When your inner creative genius is urging you to take a risk, but you're afraid of how others might view it, this creates a standstill inside of you. You become stuck in indecision between the forces pulling you in two different directions.

But remember what we talked about a few chapters ago: it takes more energy to stay in doubt than it does to move in either direction. The energy it takes to procrastinate by deliberating between one choice and the other can be draining because you are constantly asking, "Well, what if I did this? Or what if I did that?" You are effectively ping-ponging between the two, constantly preparing your nervous system for one and then the other.

When you're in a performance or an audition, having the habit of indecision can be disastrous. Even in something highly scripted and rehearsed, you are constantly faced with small choices in the moment. Perhaps another musician makes a mistake, or the director asks you to take on a new challenge in the scene, and you are forced to make choices and to do so wholeheartedly. If you're living in the fear of having made the wrong choice, then you're not living in the moment.

When we take into account what everyone else thinks, we can become paralyzed with information. But when we look only to that one true voice inside of us, the one that feels passion and excitement, then the answer is always clear and the desire to move forward urgent and necessary.

Blame, Anger, Hatred, Bigotry, and Competitiveness

It's easier to be angry at someone when you see them as different than you. The fear of the other breeds misunderstandings and ultimately leads to anger and hate. We cannot hate that which we know and understand, because to know and understand something is to become intimate with it and, ultimately, to feel compassion for it.

The world thrives on its diversity and differences, and they should be celebrated. But when we are steeped in the fear of the other, we are focused on the differences as an object of concern. Instead of seeking to learn more about the other and to understand those differences, we are allowing them to cement as hard-and-fast truths, not allowing for the experience of the individual. We connect to a stereotype instead of connecting to an individual. We become more attached to the integrity of our pre-determined way of looking at things than we are to the integrity of our interpersonal experiences.

Ultimately, all of this creates competitiveness. If there is separation, then there is cause to worry about the outcome of us vs. them. There is less initiative in working together and creating harmony if we are unsure, doubtful, or afraid of the other that we are coming together with. And so the alternative is to pit against, to compete, and to use the other as an excuse to for our own lack, our own feelings of not enoughness. We drain our resources worrying about "them" rather than generating love by understanding "them."

Feelings of Being an Outsider

I've worked with artists and their fears for over a decade now, and what I've come to understand is that most artists feel like outsiders among outsiders. Even when they're in a community of other like-minded, risk taking, creative individuals, artists will often feel like they don't belong.

> In this way the fear of the other manifests as the worry of not belonging. We are tribal creatures, meant to lean on one another and co-exist in community. We can't do it all alone. Often, an artist's feelings of being an outsider in society will begin to form a general sense of being left out, even among other artists.

Sometimes it's almost worn as a badge of honor: the lone-wolf syndrome. The outsider goes their own route and doesn't answer to anyone. They forge their own path and identify themselves in their unwillingness to confine themselves to the norms of society. They bravely seek out the road less travelled and question (or even mock) those who are too willing to conform in order to fit in. But, in fact, even in the proud claim of being an outsider there is always a relationship to the other. You begin to define yourself and what is outside based on the other who is inside.

When the fear of the other manifests as identifying as an outsider, the implications extend far beyond loneliness or isolation—they threaten our very survival. This is why, back in the day, the threat of excommunication from the church or your community held such a powerful sway.

The pull to be a part of community is powerful, but those of us who have been traumatized by our experiences with it can often feel a repulsion to connecting with others. The shadow self jumps in to protect you. Having an autonomous identity—being different, special, on the fringes of society—are of utmost importance to this shadow part of you. And when prodded to connect with others, it can feel like the very essence of your artistic persona on is being challenged.

Thus, we now learn about our very first shadow self: meet the Outlaw.

Signs That You Are Allowing The Fear Of The Other To Run You

You find yourself thinking biting comments about others even if you don't say them. You tend to feel like you're "tuned in" and can read what others think about you. You worry what others think. You judge them harshly because, in your mind, they are probably judging you. You keep track of your position in relationship to other artists. You have a propensity for worshiping those you admire and may act differently or not feel like yourself around them. You are highly self-critical. You often find yourself thinking that others are to blame for your problems. You often feel left out. In your mind, you are often dwelling on others and making up stories about what they're thinking.

Your Shadow Self: The Outlaw

The shad... other is ... of the

When I w...
screamir...
just sh...
Outla...
muc'...
att...

...ryone crying, ...d everyone to ...e people!" The ..., thank you very ...on and need for

...e from the time we ...playing outside the ..., for great art, but it ...ıber of society. Many ...oughout our lives, and ...e accessed the Outlaw

...ınity, roams wildly, does
as they ...   ...ic or even unlawful. They
don't exist w...   ...ıd out of ıt as they please. Outlaws are
bringers of chaos, a...   ...of justice that falls outside of society's
definition.

The Outlaw is often seen as ... ,exy because as much as they are a bane to society, they are also "wanted." Special, elusive, recognizable. These are things that the Outlaw doesn't want to give up. They know the moment they accept the invitation to step inside community, then things will get intimate, complicated, and much harder for them to control. The ultimate goal of the Outlaw is maintaining identity and freedom. As much as the Outlaw relies on the norm in order to defy it, they also fear the oneness, the loss of identity, and the loss of freedom.

Creatively, the Outlaw attempts to depend on no one else. As a result, they want you to be milder in your expectations, cooler in regards to success, praise, and rewards. They don't want to be caught off guard or manipulated by false

"To me, an outlaw is a man that did things his own way, either you liked him or not. I did things my own way."

– Johnny Paycheck

compliments, and so their knee-jerk response is to deflect them. What keeps them moving is the sunset, something just out of reach on the horizon, a future fountain of energy they can never quite connect with. Whereas the Rebel can get behind a cause, the Outlaw is primarily only looking out for themselves. Deep down they just don't trust anyone else.

Appeasing The Outlaw:	They can connect with other outlaws on the road, and in fact, they are happiest in small groups or one-on-one around the fire at night. Their natural distrust of others and ability to draw their firearm quickly can sometimes be an advantage to keep everyone safe in the right context. They may even find themselves leading groups of other outlaws at some point, like Robin Hood and his band of thieves.
Important to The Outlaw:	Individuality, alone time, freedom, easy escape routes
How The Outlaw Handles Fear:	With stoicism, their strength is their connection to self; by fleeing, where they try to outrun their pursuer; occasionally in a stand-off but they're more likely to dodge a bullet or disappear when your back is turned than they are to actually fight.
Admired for:	Their elusiveness, mystery, toughness, seemingly cool detachment from what others think.
The Outlaw says:	"You can't catch me," "Goodbye," "I don't need these people," "I don't care what they think."
Famous Outlaws:	Robin Hood, Butch Cassidy, Annie Oakley, Mata Hari, every cowboy ever

"When freedom is outlawed, only outlaws will be free."
– Tom Robbins

Your Love & Fear Elixir: In what ways do you relate to the Outlaw? In what parts of your life do you run away from the masses and flee to the sunset? When are you stoic? Mysterious? Feeling like an outcast? What are you on the outside of, exactly? What is it that the Outlaw in you is rejecting?

Connection: Plugging Into Your Power

It is a sunny day in Oakland, California, but Cherie does not feel sunny. Alone in her little apartment, she has no reason to brush her teeth first thing in the morning, but she does. She does not like the idea of going into a dentist's office or any doctor's office right now, not with the potential germs running amok in the city. No COVID cavities for me, she thinks ruefully. After brushing, she aimlessly finds herself on social media and scrolls through people's stories with apathy. More pictures of people's gardens, more parent friends complaining about schools being shut down, some bad news, some inspiring memes—her feed is awash in an array of messages and she grows tired just looking at them, feeling even more disconnected from the world outside of her little apartment. After logging into her work computer and taking care of a few tasks, she lies down on the one patch of sunlight streaming through her eastward-facing window. She should go out for a walk. She should probably take some time to write or exercise. She should maybe think about getting a pet. But Cherie feels pretty unmotivated. She doesn't have any sense that any of it matters. She wonders if the friends she used to hang out with even miss her. She wonders when she'll be able to actually hear her work on stage again. It feels like she is floating in a sea of no outcomes, time stretching out from her in every direction, formless and unending.

When dealing with the fear of the other, there is no better place to begin than with connection. Because nothing is more important than being plugged in. Plugged in and connected to yourself, your ideas, your community, connected to the pulse of others and the vast web of humanity we're all a part of. Without connection, art has no teeth and nothing to hang on to. If we can't connect, then how can we entertain? Who would be there to listen? And what would we have to talk about? Connection, in a sense, is where it all begins.

> Without connection, art has no teeth and nothing to hang on to.

Connection is a powerful antidote to fear because it burns up this lie that fear tells us:

Other people are against me! It's like Lord of the Flies in here! Who knows what will happen next?

These fears cannot exist once a true connection has been established. Once you surrender yourself to deeply connecting with another then you are saying with every inch of your being

I trust you mean no harm.

We're all in this together.

Come with me and we'll see what happens!

Connecting in a Remote World

Unfortunately, when you're in a crisis like we are as I'm writing this—with people unable to gather in large groups, travel to see their loved ones, or in many situations, even to get a hug—then connection can seem like a very foreign and distant concept.

Even without a pandemic, connection while working in an increasingly more remote and online world can feel tough, which is why it's more important than ever to make concentrated efforts to connecting with people: your collaborators, your community, your audience, and even yourself.

But let's start with the basics. Because I know you're wondering:

How can I approach a creative project right now when I can't even get together with people?

While it's definitely different, it's not impossible. In this chapter, I'll share an example of how it can be done and how I did it.

When the pandemic hit and shelter-in-place orders happened around the world, how many things did you find yourself simply deciding to put on hold? With public venues gone and social distancing in place, you may have thought to yourself, Well, doing that collaborative project seems impossible right now. . . I guess I'll pick it up later. And over the duration of the quarantine you may have given yourself a (no doubt) long-deserved break. Maybe you found yourself cleaning out your closet, planting a garden, taking up new hobbies or solo creative endeavors.

And now, as the pandemic stretches on, and we aren't seeing a return to "normal" anytime soon . . . you may be wondering,

What about those creative things I wanted to do? Are they paused indefinitely? Will I ever get to create in collaboration again?

I recently directed a piece with twenty dancers living separately all over the West Coast—most of whom had never met each other, some of whom even I had never even met—in a dance collaboration. What started as a response to shelter-in-place orders ended up as a film that speaks and reflects the times and movements we're living. It's a timepiece, and it turned out even better than I imagined . . .

. . . and it wouldn't have been possible if I hadn't asked the right questions.

Instead of asking, "will I ever create?" I asked,

"How can I create?"

Here's the thing: we don't know when—if ever—we'll return to "normal" or what that new normal will even look like. We don't know if the pandemic ends, what's to follow, what world events we're going to encounter next.

But we can find new ways of working together when we ask the right questions.

Here are some of the important keys and the questions that helped me in connecting remotely.

Maintain Momentum

> **Ask yourself: In what ways can I keep the momentum going and keep people engaged?**

I think one of the biggest challenges when working apart is keeping the momentum and enthusiasm going. When people aren't seeing each other in person, it can be all too easy to detach, tune out the email reminders, and fall off the radar.

How I handled it:

At the very onset of the project, each person had to fill out a simple Google Form to let me know they wanted to do be a part of the project. I created a private Facebook group with all these dancers where everyone was encouraged to share ideas and inspiration. Then I had a kickoff meeting. We had about 50% attendance on this, so I made sure to record it and make it available for everyone.

Another big thing was I made sure the dancers had a very short time in which to add to the project and turn in their dance video contribution. They had only two days, and I let it be known that they had to either commit to that or let me know they needed to "pass" and I would come back to them later. This served two purposes: there could be no extreme amounts of procrastination or getting blocked by perfectionism. They had to go with their gut, get out to a location, try a few things, and get it done. This made the project feel finite.

The Outlaw in you is doing great in any situation that distances you from others. Living barebones, catching their own fish, and eating all the s'mores. You can really let your Outlaw run the show for a while. They were made for solitude, but eventually, even the Outlaw gets lonely.

Also, as soon as I assigned the project to the next dancer, I announced it to the group. Every few dancers, I would post the latest version of the video. In this way, the entire group could see that the project was moving forward, the film was getting made, and it helped them get excited about the result.

Remember that working apart is like having a long-distance relationship. You have to keep the romance alive!

Encourage Self-Direction

Ask yourself: How do I direct people to direct themselves and also support them from afar?

If people aren't in the room together when they're collaborating, then that means you have to find ways to empower them to make their own aesthetic decisions. Communicate the vision clearly enough that it's easy to follow, with room to interpret and play and allow for some personal authority over the result. You also should mentally prepare people for creating alone.

Filming yourself dancing in public is a little embarrassing no matter how many times you do it. You always have to remind yourself that you're doing something meaningful even though you feel like onlookers are probably thinking you're just some egomaniac with an iPhone. Also, choreography that looks good in your living room doesn't necessarily work the way you think once you are onsite. You may find that the only good light is available at 6:30 a.m., meaning that you have to move your body, in public, in an artistic way at a very non-optimal time of day. There are countless challenges when trying to create something out in the world by yourself—one of the main ones being mentally prepared and maintaining your self-esteem.

The Outlaw is saying, "I was made for these times!" And "I knew this would happen!"

How I handled it:

I gave people very clear specifications on what I was asking for. They knew how to film their dance from the position of the camera, to the length of the clip, to the logistics of getting it to me afterwards. As a group, we discussed lighting, locations, costumes, and we watched inspiring videos together. They got this information in meetings, and then again in posts, and then again in a text message when I was handing off the project. I always let them know I was available any time they were in the middle of shooting and needed a second eye.

All with the idea in mind that I was prepping them for that inevitable moment when they would feel a little lonely out on their own. I was instilling confidence in them to direct themselves. A couple of times I received calls or a timid text with a video, "Do you think this is ok?" In almost every instance, they were totally on the right track, but I think just knowing someone else was seconding their opinion helped them to feel supported.

Build bridges between the artists and their original inspiration for creating so they feel supported when no one else is there.

And with the Dancing Together Apart project, I began to notice that not only did it work really well to collaborate remotely, it was actually easier in some ways. Normally, a dance company would have to rent studio time, rehearse together, make schedules together, invest more time and money just to be able to work together. We were all busy women with families and/or careers, so being able to choose when we created and doing it in our own space was not only workable but turned out to be a luxurious experience.

The entire world became our dance studio and artistic playground: murals, beaches, forests, tunnels. Places we used to just walk through now we saw with new eyes. The world around us—ugly, beautiful, turbulent and peaceful—all of it became a rich storehouse for our imaginations and dances.

In a time when we could have all felt stuck, hopeless, lonely, or ineffective, we were instead feeling connected, creative, and proactive. We were finding new inspiration inside our limitations.

As the world was waking up to the terrifying spaces between us in regards to race and the Black Lives Matter movement, we were finding ways to mend our own. We were creating closeness inside the separation and recognizing the need and desire in every human to be able to create together and also apart.

Your Love & Fear Elixir: What are the things that you miss right now? What have you had to give up recently or adjust to? What have you lost? Before we can move onto the solution it sometimes helps to name those things that we are grieving.

Now what?

Ask yourself, in what ways can I connect?

How can I engage people, empower them, and support them? How can I create a sense of connection even in a remote-working situation?

Holly Shaw

Your Creative Community

As a young dancer, I felt awkward in my dance community, out-of-place from the popular girls and always just outside of the group. In my experience coaching, listening, interviewing, working with hundreds of artists over the years, I have discovered that I am not alone in this experience. In short, artists are a bunch of loners. We often feel like the outsiders even within our own artistic communities. It is something that can give us a type of strength when we're younger—it can help us not to care too much what others think and give us time alone to ruminate, dream, and work on our art—but if it leaks into our adult lives, it can weaken our ability to make strides in our artistic pursuits. Because nothing great is ever done completely alone.

The stereotype of the artist as the outsider, the loner, the mad genius is commonplace in film and media across many cultures, and many artists can relate to having grown up feeling that way. Because we were often a little "different," we were often made fun of, ridiculed, left out because of our weirdness or "too-much-ness." Often, artists don't find community until later in life. And while that time spent alone may have served us when we were younger, as we get older, it becomes less of a help and more of a hindrance when it comes to taking our ideas out of our heads and into the world.

We don't create anything entirely alone in a bubble. In fact, in many cases, it has become evident that the success of your career as an artist depends less on your originality or your talent and more on how connected you are. In fact, "The Art of Fame," a research paper published by Columbia Business School, reported that "those individuals [who] possessed a diverse set of personal friends and professional contacts from different industries (an artist in a 'cosmopolitan' network position) were statistically more likely to become famous." In short, we need people to succeed. Every artist who has ever felt like the outsider has had to work through these feelings to some degree in order to find their people and become successful.

If we are actually going to live and create and move past our fear of the other, we have to recognize that things like making a name for ourselves and making it to the top aren't about scrambling over others. Instead of beating someone out,

> *"Circumstances have forced us to become what we are-outcasts and outlaws-and as bad as we are, we are not so bad as we are supposed to be."*
>
> – Ned Kelly

think of it as simply leading the way for others. Your community plays a huge role in this ascension. Are you part of one? Do they have your back? And what have you done for them or do for them now?

Over the years, I've been a part of many different communities: several dance communities, the SAG/AFTRA union acting community, festival communities that come together once a year, parent communities where you become friends with parents simply because your kids like to play together, coaching communities that see each other for events and gather a lot online, the comedy community where you see the same forty people all the time at open mics ... And in each one, I would say I played a different role.

For a very long time, I continued the pattern of feeling on the "outside" of every group. That feeling would lead to being less engaged, less committed, in some cases, even snarky or critical of the way a group was led. The benefit of being on the outside is you allow yourself to criticize those who are on the inside. If you aren't "in it," then you can always claim that you would do it better. It's an easy out. A simple shrugging off of responsibility. Over the years, that pattern repeated in areas of my life until I started to really see it for what it was. Only then did I make a conscious effort to start showing up differently. And now being a leader of the Performers & Creators Lab Community, I can say that I participate very differently in community than I used to. I show up better. I don't expect more than I put in. I criticize others less and try to learn and build upon what others are doing instead of tearing it down.

We have this fantasy that an artist comes up with their ideas alone, but in fact, having other creatives to bounce ideas often makes for some of the best work. Collaboration like this has given birth to entire genres of music, of art, of styles, and shaped generations.

So, if you're feeling stuck or uninspired in your creations, start by looking around. What artistic communities are you a part of? What role do you play in those communities? And what resentments do you have?

If we are truly going to task ourselves with making art in the middle of madness, then that means finding the non-madness in there. Finding the places we can trust others, feel received, share ideas and be witnessed. The peaceful pockets.

"Love is the ultimate outlaw. It just won't adhere to any rules. The most any of us can do is sign on as its accomplice."

– Tom Robbins

Community Deep Dive

Answer these questions to reveal what type of roles you've been playing in your communities and get insights into how you can show up better:

- List all the communities (artistic and others) you are a part of.
- Next to each one, specify what kind of role you play. Are you a leader, a member, an organizer, an instigator, a quiet judge?
- How do you engage? How do you not engage? Have you given yourself rules for engagement? (i.e., in my professional groups or with other parents I don't normally talk about my sex life, but with my close girlfriends we often talk candidly about love affairs)
- What do you share? What do you keep to yourself?
- How do you add to the group?
- What does the group add to your life?
- What have you learned from this community? What do you love about it?
- What resentments do you have about this community? What bugs you about it?
- What was the trajectory of your membership in that group (i.e., did you start out on the fringes and work your way in)?
- What commitments did you make to this group (tacitly or openly)? Did you hold to those commitments?
- Look for any patterns across these groups. Do you have similar patterns of resentments across all of them? Do you only belong to groups you can lead? Do you always stay on the outer sphere of the group?

Just like we don't get everything from one partner or person in life, the same is true of community —we go to different groups for different things. That being said, some groups we stay in as an active member for a while, and then it is time to move on. Perhaps the group is no longer serving us, or we aren't aligned with their mission anymore, or we have simply found other groups that make more sense to be a part of. It's ok to have multiple communities in your life, and sometimes, you may need to move on from one completely. It's good to make space for something new, whether you're creating a community or finding one to be a part of.

Your Love & Fear Elixir: After looking deeply at all the communities you've been a part of and all of these patterns, ask yourself, what are you missing? Maybe all of your communities are short-lived. Maybe you're looking for something longer lasting. Or maybe through this exercise you've come face-to-face with the realization that you've stayed in something that's not working for you far too long. Whatever your situation, use this community deep dive to help you pinpoint what you've created for yourself and whether you're leading it or simply a member. Either way, start taking an active role in making your communities ones you want to be a part of.

Excommunication & Exclusion

From when we are socialized as little kids in school, we learn about community. Be nice. Be fair. Share your toys. Don't hit. Do unto others. . . And throughout much of our young lives, we are made to fit into the communities around us—in school, church, kids on our block—whether they suit us or not, whether we feel comfortable or accepted there or not. It's only when a young person branches out freely into the world for the first time as an adolescent—first through college or those years after high school, then through the workplace, hobbies, social activities—that we begin to intentionally pick our communities.

And we aren't always so great at it.

Sometimes we pick some real stinkers. Or we pick people who seem great at first but who don't see us and accept us as fully as we require.

Given that we didn't have a lot of freedom to choose when we were little, it makes sense that we're kind of bad at choosing our communities at first. You go with friends to a party because they invite you and you're bored. You try this activity out because it's where people are going, only later to discover you've found yourself in the company of people you don't enjoy or are quickly outgrowing.

Hey, you've got wings, and when it's time to fly off, it's just time!

Nevertheless, endings can be hard. Falling out with one friend can sometimes mean leaving an entire community behind. Outgrowing certain behaviors may put you outside a circle that once was yours, and they may even excommunicate you. I've even seen situations where trauma or abuse can separate the victim from the very community that should be there to support them.

This should be recognized as something to grieve. All too often we get the advice to just push through it, or to forget those people and move on! But in in these situations it's often unclear what we're moving on to, and so we find ourselves in solitude for periods of time.

This is a natural part of growing as a human. Not everyone is going to grow with you or be conducive to your growth. Leaving people or whole communities

"Grief, I've learned, is really just love. It's all the love you want to give, but cannot. All that unspent love gathers up in the corners of your eyes, the lump in your throat, and in that hollow part of your chest. Grief is just love with no place to go."

– Jamie Anderson

behind is not only OK, but in some ways, it is imperative to your lifelong process of becoming an artist.

In those stark open spaces where you may feel like you're flying without the "safety net" of a group, just remember that grieving is normal. It's OK to feel sad at the loss of what you thought you had. Just know that more people are coming and the opportunities to collaborate with exciting new people are on their way . . . now that your calendar is wide open.

Don't Expect Your Peers To Be Your Audience

It took me a long time to truly understand this. For years as a dancer and an actor, I worked for respect and attention from my peers, and it hurt when I wasn't recognized or included in certain projects. But what I didn't understand at the time was that I had my focus pointed entirely in the wrong direction. I was performing for the wrong people. Years of my career, creative productivity, and energy were siphoned off trying to please others or getting bogged down in group politics. It's easy to do. It's natural to want to be "in community" with like-minded people doing similar things, but in my experience, you'll find just a handful here or there that are actually cheering for you.

Can I get honest with you? Your peers are not your audience . . . they are other people trying to do the same thing you are, and they may or may not be genuinely rooting for you. Instead of looking side to side or worrying about what everyone else is doing, focus on connecting with your real audience (hint: it's not other artists) and "doing you" as best as you can. Along the way, you will find a handful of artistic "soulmates" who truly get you and are invested in your success.

Your Love & Fear Elixir: Where have you experienced excommunication or exclusion? Who have you relied on, only to be let down or disappointed? Looking back on your experiences in community, where were you a part of the breakdown of trust? Being honest with yourself, ask yourself, when did I not fully support another artist? When have I secretly not cheered them on allowing the fear of the other to go unchecked in my own heart?

"The difference between a criminal and an outlaw is that while the criminals frequently are victims, outlaws never are. Indeed, the first step toward becoming a true outlaw is the refusal to be victimized."

– Tom Robbins

Collaborators: Your Creative Soulmates

While we may be part of a wider group of people in a community, it is our collaborators who we need to trust even more.

Collaborators are people you choose to not only share the artistic path with but also people with whom you can share your deep ideas in their infancy. These trusted people might wear your work, dance your work, or become a part of your work. Collaborators are often your most trusted advisors. They are the people who you can call up on any given day because you're bursting with an idea and they answer the phone, hungry to hear what's on your mind. Collaborators are golden. I often wonder if they're connected to us on a soul level. In short, collaborators pick up what you're puttin' down.

Five Signs of a Creative Soulmate:

1. When you call them, they're excited to hear from you. They call you back. They touch in.

2. Their enthusiasm matches your own. They are almost as excited as you are about your next project.

3. They're interested in your work even if it doesn't involve them. They're able to set their ego aside and simply be happy for you.

4. You serve them and they serve you. There is reciprocity, generosity, and helpfulness from both sides and you feel no need to keep track because you find it just naturally feels equal and balanced.

5. You'll work with them more than once. . . And usually in more than one way. Creative soulmates often continue to circle around each other over decades, even switching

roles: you learn from them and they learn from you; some-times you are directing and other times it's the opposite. It hardly matters with a creative soulmate. There's so much respect that you're simply happy to be collaborating—the hierarchical structure doesn't factor much into your enjoyment of the sparks that fly when you're together.

Your Love & Fear Elixir: Who are your creative soulmates? Make a list of people you've worked with over the years. Are there any who came up more than once? Who are the people who "get" you or with whom you feel like you have an unspoken understanding? Make it a point to spend time with at least one creative soulmate a week. It will be good for both of you.

Connecting with Your Crowd

How often have you practiced a scene or a number in your head, but when the time comes to deliver on stage, it's nothing like what you expected? How many times have you imagined the response you might receive on social media to your next "sure to be viral" post, only to have it feel completely different once you hit that 'post' button? Maybe it falls flat or isn't received as you had hoped. It's a complete disconnect.

In any kind of performance situation, your audience becomes a co-collaborator. Like it or not, they are players in the act. With nothing more than their energetic presence, your audience becomes part of the show. While this may seem less so in digital media, T.V., or film, where the art is made in advance and then shared with an audience later, it's still an imagined audience that involves itself in the artist making the work. There is still the response and feedback from the people you are interacting with, even if it is delayed.

Your audience has a prominent role in the performance. Paying attention to that interaction—to that invisible cord of energy that flows between you and them—is paramount to not only becoming the best performer possible, but also to making the whole situation of putting yourself out in the public eye less scary for yourself.

We can debate ad nauseum about all the different ways we can affect our audience, make an impact, craft our content—and yet it all means nothing, total diddly squat, without first creating connection and bridging that gap between you and your audience.

Getting Your Audience to Trust You

Have you ever reached out to a child you've just met for the first time and watched them close off to you? Children are trusting mostly, but more often they are just plain honest. If they don't know you or trust you, they may be outright unfriendly—and let you know it!

And so, I'd invite you to imagine your audience is like a little child. It's a safe bet to assume you'll have to earn their trust before they'll go with you on a journey through your show/art/expression or even pay attention. This trust-building

"If your audience doesn't trust you, if they don't feel safe that you're carrying the music for them, then they can't open up and receive the story that you're telling them."

– Terrance Kelly, Emmy award winning director of the Oakland Interfaith Gospel Choir

happens in small moments of reinforcement and integrity within your story— your vulnerability, the way in which you build and use tension—all things which we're covering in these next few chapters.

The Most Powerful Person In the Room

The Outlaw wants to be trustworthy to their chosen few: they talk about ideas and not people; they keep others' secrets and they safeguard their own.

Once this trust is established, a beautiful thing begins to unfold: The audience lets go and allows themselves to step into your experience. Through their attention and awareness of you, they inevitably surrender to your story and, provided that you also surrender yourself to the present moment of your performance...

You become the most powerful person in the room!

The audience syncs up with you and together you travel through one energetic shared space, with you at the helm. And so, if you reach an ecstatic state, guess what that means? Yep, you betcha! Your audience can have the potential to feel it too. If you trance out, they trance out. They and you—all of you—have become entranced.

Understanding Entrainment

Have you ever wondered why two pendulums sitting next to each other that are swinging at different times will eventually synchronize? It's because of a concept called entrainment.

Entrainment is a concept first identified by the Dutch physicist Christiaan Huygens in 1665 who discovered the phenomenon during an experiment with pendulum clocks: He set them each in motion and found that when he returned the next day, the sway of their pendulums had all synchronized.

Such entrainment occurs because small amounts of energy are transferred between the two systems when they are out of phase in such a way as to produce negative feedback. As they assume a more stable phase relationship, the amount of energy gradually reduces to zero, with systems of greater frequency slowing down, and the other speeding up. Wikipedia

In essence, entrainment refers to a natural phenomenon in which one entity resonates synchronously with another in response to its dominant frequency of vibration.

You Go First and Then They Follow. . .

Here's a little something I learned as a hypnotherapist: Trance states will tend to be matched by those around you.

I know this because every time I put a client into a trance, I tend to go into a mild trance myself. I allow this because I know that if I go, then they will follow. As human beings, we feed off community, interaction, and connection—and as a result, we tend to entrain with each other. We meet each other on the playing field of the mind and spirit. We literally go on conscious or subconscious journeys with each other.

What does this mean for you, creator? Performing artist?

It means that if you go there, so too will the audience. When you have a crowd of people all fixated on you, up there with the lights pointed at you, then you naturally become the most charged person in the room. Now, you can also do all kinds of things to dissipate this charge. Things that undermine your performance, break trust, or create a disconnect between you and your audience. But if you use that attention and that charge that you are getting and wield it wisely, continuing to foster that connection, the audience will naturally entrain with you. It's physics. It's LAW.

> Trance states tend to be matched by those around you. If you let yourself be entranced, then so goes your audience.

And that's why when we use these techniques properly, we have an ability to take people on a journey.

There is a shift in reality when people view your work. When you as an artist say look at me, or you call in an audience, when you stand up and speak in a crowd, there is the beginning of a transcendent state. By listening to you, people are saying, "All right, we agree to go with you . . . Maybe we aren't committed to the full ride yet, but we will commit to listening to you in this moment." The masterful performer knows this on some level and doesn't take the audience's trust lightly. They seize that moment of surrender, of willingness of vulnerability and uses it to their and the audience's advantage - stretching it out and using that moment to win your trust.

And when we are being held by that level of shared trust, any leftover fear simply flies out the window.

The question is, how do we get that trust from the audience? How do we entice them to come along for the journey and convince them to stay once they're on it? We use two of the most important hallmarks of riveting performances: vulnerability and tension.

Vulnerability

One of the things that makes live performance so thrilling is the element of vulnerability and risk. I want to see some daring involved. Someone taking chances, whether it is an aspect of the work that is improvised or the performer being emotionally open with the audience. Vulnerability.

A fear that often crops up among performers is that if they become too vulnerable or real, then they might lose themselves, or lose control. I've counseled artists who were afraid of crying or losing control onstage, but more often the anxiety manifests itself more subtly in things like tight movements, inexpressive faces, or well-executed but non-moving performances. Audiences are smart. They can feel when the person on stage has too tight a grip on what's going on. Remember our little talk about entrainment? Your audience isn't as moved if the performer isn't moved—and when this happens, the performances might be good, just not great.

Here's the thing about vulnerability:

When you are vulnerable, you allow others to see themselves in you. You become their hero. When you persist, so do they. When you go through a catharsis, so do they. Through you they also get to win.

But it isn't always easy to let down our guard. When we're asked to bare our truest self, our Outlaw looks at us with disdain. We have to ask them to stop reaching for their gun and leave their hands at their sides. It's scary. There's a part of us that is afraid of being vulnerable when the proverbial guns start blazing, but we have to remember these shots, though they might sting a bit, won't kill us. We're dealing with water guns and nerf guns, not real ones.

Over years of observing performers—as well as putting myself in the hot seat onstage—I've determined some useful tools that performing artists can use in order to allow for authenticity, while at the same time, soothing their anxiety about it. Here are some ways that you can increase your tolerance and adeptness at vulnerability while at the same time feeling a little less out of control.

How to Be Vulnerable On Stage Without Losing Your Shit

Use Movement to Evoke Emotions not the other way around

There are many ways "up the mountain" when it comes to creating and performing art, but in order to clearly illustrate my point, let's simplify and talk about only two approaches: You can either feel an emotion and then take action from the emotion, or you can begin with the action, using different movements to elicit an emotional response (e.g., using variation of speed, texture, levels, specificity, timing, etc.). Both approaches are valid and work well in different situations, but for purposes of alleviating your anxiety about "being vulnerable," it would do you well to approach what you are doing by focusing your thoughts and interest on your actions first, then allow your emotions to arise and unfold from there.

The body is a powerful messenger to the brain. Do something with your body, and your emotions will fall into line. This can be understood easily by simply smiling or frowning. Try crying artificially: scrunch up your face in a grimace, slope your shoulders forward, make some heaving crying sounds, and it doesn't take too long until you actually start to feel sad and really cry. Now lift your shoulders up and back, relax your face, take a deep breath, tilt your chin upwards and let the corners of your lips lift in a smile. Don't you feel better? It is helpful to know that your body can elicit an emotional response. Once you understand this, you can manipulate your emotions through moving your body.

If you choose the other approach, you will focus on some story or image in your head—especially if it pertains to a memory of an actual personal event—in order to elicit an emotional response before the movement. At that point, your body can flip into a "flight or fight" mode and your instinct could be to freeze up and stop moving altogether. It depends on what emotional response you are working with in your piece, but if you are anxious about losing the ability to move, then start with the moving, not the memory.

> When we talk about getting vulnerable, our inner Outlaw begins losing their shit! Why the hell would I want to be vulnerable?

Look for the Eyes

Look for the eyes of your audience members. Are you lucky enough to be onstage with someone else? Great. Look into their eyes. It is simple but effective. There is something truly grounding about connecting to another human being. Uncomfortable or not used to doing this? Ok, then just begin by trying it out everywhere, in art and life: do it in grocery stores, do it with your co-workers. Look deeply into the eyes of your children, spouse, friends. My favorite actor, Amy Poehler, says it best in her Harvard commencement speech*: "If you are scared, look into your partner's eyes. You'll feel better."

So why is this so hard? For one thing, we don't gaze into someone's eyes nearly often enough. There is the fear that you will be perceived as strange or creepy or you'll make someone uncomfortable. But there's also another reason.

Sometimes you're afraid to see others seeing you.

When you look into someone else's eyes, then like it or not, you will start getting a read of how they feel in this moment. They become a part of the performance. They affect you. The trick is to take this feedback as a reaction to the moment as opposed to a reaction or feeling they have about you. They could be furrowing their eyebrows because they're intrigued by what they're watching, or they could be annoyed by the way you speak. They might look bored because that's just how their face is! Not because you are boring. Basically, you don't know one way or the other. It may in fact be about you, but in that moment, it doesn't matter! You have to believe they are having their own personal reaction to this moment. You have a job to do. Now isn't the time to take it personally.

When you're able to do this—to make it about the moment and not about you—then you'll find you can be more porous, you can take in the response, and you can even choose to respond or incorporate it without throwing yourself into self-judgement or weaving a story that's not helpful. You can see them seeing you and stay present.

Learn to Move from General to Specific—and Back Again

Start working with the tool of going from general ideas to specific ideas and then back again to general ideas. It works like this: the more specific in details you get, the more intense the emotions you evoke; but the more general your thoughts, the more you slow down the emotional momentum.

If you want to really tug on your emotions, then get specific about the details of what you've created for yourself. Actors know this. Good actors like to prepare themselves for their work by creating a whole world of details about their character's life and thoughts. Sometimes they will even journal as though they are that character. This is often understood to be the "lonely work" of acting. What this does is it gives actors a whole host of details to draw from when they are becoming that character on stage. The minutiae make it "real" to them so they can live the part, as opposed to "acting" the part.

Specificity is a great tool to dig in with, but it also works the other way around. If you are performing and feel yourself getting strung too deeply into a dark role, you can always back away by allowing your thoughts to be more general and thus slow down the intensity. With practice, you can do this without sacrificing the authenticity.

Wait Until the Last Moment to Get "Into It"

Another way to manage being vulnerable is to put a time limit on it. It doesn't take all day to conjure up an emotion and it's best to not expect yourself to stay in character or in that frame of mind required for your performance more than you need to. This works because then you have a container - you don't have to be vulnerable all the time. Just on stage.

I recently watched an interview with Angelina Jolie on Inside The Actors Studio, in which she describes this lesson so perfectly. She says that if she had a really emotional scene to shoot that day, she would wake up and immediately start thinking about it. This would affect the way that she treated those around her, making her feel pulled in two directions as she navigated between having her head in the scene while at the same time wanting to be able to function with others. She said that by the time it was time to shoot the scene, she would have a headache from all the mental gymnastics she was putting herself through. Finally, she learned that it was much better if she made sure she had a really good day and left the mental preparation for the fifteen minutes beforehand.

This is a good lesson for all performers. Don't exhaust yourself mentally ahead of time! Imagining the performance is an important tool, and I would not dissuade anyone from using it—and yet there is something to be said for preparing and then giving yourself a rest. Let it breathe, let it go. If you've taken yourself there in practice, if you've put in your rehearsal time, then it is best to leave your emotional resources for the final few moments before stage time.

Lose Your Shit and See What Happens

Do the thing you're afraid of. Take advantage of small audiences, low-pressure performances, classes where the vibe is comfortable, rehearsal time, etc. If you can push yourself beyond your limits a little when others aren't watching or when the pressure is low, then you'll be able to experience whatever it is you're afraid of. Maybe you will cry, fall, look wonderfully ghastly with snot dripping down your face—but you'll have the opportunity to take the zing out of the fear.

You may discover it isn't so scary after all.

Lean In Harder

That's right. Throw yourself into it headfirst. It seems counter-intuitive to what you might want to do when you're scared, but that is just the point. You can't be scared and committed at the same time. For the longest time, I thought that I had a fear of being vulnerable onstage, but I've come to realize that it isn't the vulnerability that frightens me at all. It's the going halfway that horrifies me. I'm afraid of the mediocrity that happens on stage when I want to be doing something emotionally poignant, but I'm not able to pull it off. True emotional vulnerability onstage is riveting. But if you take a step back, or shrink from it in any way, then it melts into tepid melodrama and self-judgement. Audiences are smart—they feel the difference. There is no way around it, no tool to fix it, no mask to wear—authenticity is simply commitment. Commitment to the movement in front of you. To the story you are telling. Commitment to being right here, right now.

Ultimately, your vulnerable authentic self is all there is to see. These suggestions are meant to give you tools to soothe your anxiety, but the idea that you

Ultimately, your vulnerable authentic self is all there is to see.

have control is a bit of an illusion. Once you get up on stage, it is all about trusting yourself fully. If you are lucky, you might actually fall all the way in and really "lose" yourself to something bigger. If you're lucky.

Your Love & Fear Elixir: When do you find it hard to be vulnerable, open, or honest? Look beyond the stage: Where in your life do you find it tough to open up? With whom and on what topics? See if you notice any patterns between your artistic vulnerability and your personal vulnerability. Is there any connection?

"The fear of criticism robs man of his initiative, destroys his power of imagination, limits his individuality, takes away his self-reliance, and does him damage in a hundred other ways."

– Napoleon Hill, Think and Grow Rich

Tension

Seven members of the band stand in a line across the stage, reminding me of an army of superheroes, strong and unflinching. They had been announced one by one onto the stage, and now they stand motionless while a drummer and a horn player riff on a repetitive theme. The music builds tension in the room, keeping up an excited pulse but not changing. Then, all of a sudden, the music changes and all of the standing musicians slowly lean to one side in synchronicity. Then with the next phrase, they all lean to the other side, like cowboys in a standoff, leaning their bodies as though they are sizing us up. The tension continues to build with this small movement, the players synching up, the energy in the room mounting as we all wonder what is going to happen next. Finally, the tension breaks as the musicians all dash in different directions, grab their instruments, and explode into music. The song takes off, the singer launches into a dance, and the audience goes with them.

The band was Monsieur Periné performing at the San Francisco Jazz Center, and that performance—and particularly that moment at the beginning—stands out in my mind as a powerful example of how performers use tension. Just as much as you need the trust of an audience, you also need some tension in the room. You want them to be willing to go with you, but also be alert. Entranced, but not sleepy. You want them to trust you, but you want them on the edge of their seats because they don't know where you're taking them next.

Tension is the space of the unexpected. It's the energetic charge that increases when the audience doesn't know what's going to happen next. Imagine, if you will, a rubber band running between you and your audience. Tension is the potential that grows when you stretch that rubber band. This can be done in a variety of ways—a gap of silence or stillness, or alternately an increase in volume and intensity. Tension is what creates the excitement in the room. It can make the difference between an electric performance and one that's just fine.

Tension Doesn't Exist Without Attention

Comedians are often concerned with getting laughs, sometimes as frequently as every fifteen seconds. The professionals will sometimes listen to their sets afterwards and note at which points they get laughs and count the seconds in-between. There's this idea that you have to keep the audience laughing or they'll lose interest.

One time, though, I was watching a comedian friend of mine, Roman Leo, do a set where he told a really long story that didn't start getting laughs until two or maybe three minutes into it. Afterwards, he pointed that out and said, "You'll never see me doing that at an open mic. But I felt like tonight I had the audience. I could feel they were with me and so I knew I could stretch it out and take them on a little ride before giving them the laugh. They knew they were going to laugh at some point, and so the awkwardness of the long story actually helped to build the tension."

It's no wonder that "attention" has the word "tension" inside it. When you have someone's attention, then you have the potential to build tension, to increase the aliveness in the room. But before you can ever create tension, however, you need someone to be willing to pick up the other end of the rubber band.

> The Outlaw lives for tension and excels at it. The stillness in the moments before they draw their gun, the thrill of being "wanted" of being an uncatchable figure of mystery . . . Creating tension is where the Outlaw gathers their power.

Breaking Tension

Have you ever played peek-a-boo with a baby? There's a reason why this game works with infants and toddlers. It's an example of tension. When you are hiding your face, the tension builds as they wonder where did you go? and will you ever come back? When you come into view again and say "boo," they laugh—not because you're so darn funny, but because it is a release from that fear or tension that they were experiencing.

This same device is at play in stand-up comedy. The best-case scenario is when you, the performer, create that tension with your premise or a story, and then the audience laughs when you break the tension with your punch line or a surprise twist. But I've experienced situations where I broke the tension too soon and didn't get a laugh for something that would have otherwise been funny. This could mean two jokes are too closely spaced or the rhythm of the delivery needs to be different to get both laughs.

I've also had the experience where the audience just didn't think my punch line was funny, and so the tension is still lingering. When this happens, I usually won't get a laugh unless an audience member heckles or when I say something self-deprecating about the joke. In these scenarios, the audience feels the tension and is looking for a release, but if you as the performer don't provide it, then it will surface in other (less-desirable) ways.

You will build and break tension many times throughout the course of your performance. When an audience member says that they were "entranced," "immersed," or "couldn't take their eyes off" the performance, it is because you were able to masterfully build tension and break it—whether you were aware of it or not.

Stretching the Tension Too Far

As you're learning to play with tension as a performer, it can also happen that you can stretch that tension too far, causing your audience to either lose interest or break the tension themselves. When an audience feels that tension building and doesn't trust you to manage it, then, much to our dismay, they'll break the discomfort themselves: shifting in their seats from boredom, coughing during a pivotal death scene, laughing at a serious moment, chiming in with a joke right before you deliver your punch line. These are all signs that you were creating the tension, but you either took too long to break it or the audience doesn't quite trust you yet to manage their feelings of uneasiness.

Why It Can Be Difficult to Withstand Tension

Part of creating tension is a willingness to take up space, to be the center of attention, to allow people to wonder, to create the potential for awkwardness and aliveness to arise. This can be particularly difficult when you experience stage fright, face a confrontation, or encounter an explosive circumstance. This is especially true if you're experiencing performance anxiety that may be triggered from past traumas.

If you've ever been in a dangerous situation—a fight, an accident, or harassment of any kind—then you recognize the feeling of heightened tension from these experiences. There is a reason why tension is riveting—it's telling us there could be danger ahead. It's alerting us to be hyper-aware. For those of us who've experienced trauma or grew up in chaotic households, we learned to disperse that tension so well that we don't even realize we are doing it. Laughing, diverting attention, being self-deprecating, calming or soothing the situation, or avoiding confrontation all together—all of these are just a few ways that people learn to break the tension.

You do it for your own survival.

The ability (and desire) to break tension as soon as it arises is a really valuable skill, but it doesn't serve us on the stage, as leaders, or when we need our voices to be heard. Because we are so good at breaking tension without meaning to, we send messages that we aren't to be taken seriously (because being serious could signal the beginning of a fight), we give off alerts that we aren't a threat (because being a threat could bring us into a confrontational experience), and we divert attention away from ourselves—all of which is the exact opposite of what a performer wants to happen!

Tension is the love language of the Outlaw. In a warped way, it is their preferred method of connection.

Using Tension as an Opportunity for Change

Being the most powerful person in the room means you must learn how to take back the stage, and a big part of this begins with the very simple mechanism of learning to hold and create tension. In times of madness, it's helpful to understand that there is power in that tension—a potential for things to swing either way. Instead of being afraid of that tension, it is valuable to learn to use that charge for your benefit. If you look around you, you'll begin seeing how other people use this. News outlets use it when they promise you some upcoming "Breaking News" but keep you waiting for it. Dictators use it when they are constantly changing their message, doing disastrous things and keeping you on your toes from day to day and also keeping themselves in the headlines.

Good or bad, they've got your attention, and that's exactly what they want.

Practice Creating Tension

So, how can you start training yourself to use this mechanism of tension constructively? Below are a list of activities that are great for building tension. See where you can begin practicing these in your daily life, in conversations, in the store, with your friends, family, and in the workplace. Think of yourself as playing with that metaphorical rubber band: enjoy the stretch and then also the pop! The more you get used to playing with tension, the easier it will become to use it on stage and in crucial moments in life.

- Wait
- Linger
- Leave without explaining
- Stand still
- Be silent
- Don't answer right away
- Leave space
- Leave things unsaid
- Hold gaze
- Break out of a pattern or norm
- Do something unexpected
- Don't explain yourself
- Let someone wonder
- Repeat something
- Rule of three (do something three times, by the third there is a tension from the audience as they expect it now)

Ways You Break or Release Tension Without Even Realizing It

- Meandering or pacing on stage

- Finishing someone else's sentence

- Laughing

- Making a funny face

- Groaning or sighing

- Shifting in your seat

- Looking away from your partner's gaze

- Apologizing on stage

- Saying phrases like "I don't know... Who cares... Whatever"

- Adding vocal crutches to the end of your sentences like "you know what I mean?" instead of letting your statement stand as it is.

- Not meeting the moment (i.e., the music has built, but you just ignore the climax or muddle through it)

Your Love & Fear Elixir: When is it hard for you to build, create, or maintain tension? Where and when and with whom do you find yourself breaking tension in order to alleviate some sense of stress? Think of those moments when you have felt a good kind of tension and the *pop!* from its release. How did it make you feel? Did you feel more of a connection in those moments?

The Watermill Method:
An Exercise Using Connection to Shift Your Fear

It's all good for you to know that vulnerability and tension are important to creating connection with your audience, but how do you actually implement these things if you're riddled with self-consciousness and fear?

There are many exercises and tools in this book, but of all of these, the Watermill Exercise is one of my favorites. Not only does it help you shift your experience from fear to an ecstatic-like trance, it also helps you entrain with others. It does this by integrating all three of the things we are discussing in this book: Connection, Creativity, and Crafting Your Story; therefore, I'm sharing it with you now as something you can come back to and practice again as you read further along.

I've taught this exercise to my clients, my creative and performance laboratories, at universities, in workshops for musicians' unions, and it has been taught several times at the Screen Actors Guild Conservatory in San Francisco and Los Angeles. I've taught it to hundreds of people, and once artists use it in real life, I often get the feedback that it was the most helpful of all the things I've taught. One participant said:

> I cannot express the amount of momentum I felt after practicing the Watermill technique. I even do it if I start to get nervous about something I am thinking about going after. Yesterday I had a burst of energy and have been putting myself out there for things that I wouldn't have previously. I feel like someone took the cap off the faucet!

My recommendation is to practice this method now and start using it right away. As you work through the different sections of this book, continue to use it and see how your understanding of it changes and deepens.

Real Talk: This practice will help you in all kinds of situations and the faster you start using it, the easier and quicker it will become to do it.

Watermill Exercise

Helps with: Connecting to your audience, self-consciousness, energetic lows, lapses in audience attention, general nervousness.

When and Where This Can Be Used: On stage before you begin, or in the middle of a show if the energy slows or you feel disconnected from the audience, or before an audition in the waiting room, or in an audition before you say your first line. You can also do this exercise backstage before you begin.

Results: You'll feel more calmness, more grounded, and have the ability to think more clearly and be present in the moment.

Optimized Achievement: Connect with self, connect with audience, generate energy.

Bonus Challenge: Try this with your romantic partners! Or if you aren't in a relationship, try it with your waitress or bank teller or anyone you interact with in person. Notice how it changes your interaction with that person.

The Problem: One of the biggest things we battle when we are in the midst of fear is self-consciousness. We are overly conscious of ourselves, especially when we're on stage. Our attention is on ourselves in the least-productive manner, causing a disconnection from the situation: the room, the people in it, what's actually happening. It's like we can't see clearly—our consciousness is clouded with fear.

The Solution: In this situation, we must get the attention off ourselves and onto something or someone else. The Watermill Exercise has proven enormously helpful for actors, musicians, and speakers because it gets us out of our own heads, and therefore, out of our own way. It re-connects us with the room and helps us to use—not ignore!—the fear we're feeling. It allows us to alchemize that fear cloud into a magnetic vortex of curiosity, interest and ultimately, connection.

These five easy steps, once learned and practiced, can be used again and again before a performance or audition and at any time during the performance, especially when there is a lull. Students always ask me, "It seems like it takes a long time to do all of these steps?" But you'll find that once you know them and internalize them, these steps can be employed in a matter of seconds.

These steps can be very simply remembered like this:

Step 1. Out Step 2. In Step 3. Out Step 4. In Step 5. Out

How to Do the Five Steps of the Watermill:

Step 1. Out – Put your attention outside of yourself and observe facts

This first time that you put your attention out, you're focusing on objects, people, or things around you and noticing details in an objective manner. For example, I might look at a room and say to myself, "Five pictures hanging on the wall, gold frames, all flowers." Or if I'm looking at a scene partner, I might say to myself, "Brown eyes, black rimmed glasses, green shirt." The idea is to observe facts. Nothing subjective.

What typically happens when I teach this in workshops—especially when it's used with a scene partner—is participants will start with facts, "Green eyes, black hair," but then they will slide in subjective adjectives, "Pretty hair, smells nice."

This happens because we have a natural instinct as humans to take care of each other and say something nice, but this isn't the goal of the exercise. When doing this part of the exercise, it's important to stick to the objective observations. Here's why:

When we slide into subjective observations, (i.e., nice, pretty, good, bad, right, wrong), we turn on the part of our brain that is responsible for judgment. No matter how good our intentions are to be "nice" to our partner, this part of the mind can easily begin to turn against us, and before we know it, we can start putting the attention on ourselves and judging ourselves unkindly. Check out this example of an all-too-common thought spiral that happens when you turn on the judgment mind:

[Making inward observations of a scene partner]

Brown eyes with flecks of blue in them. . . scar on bottom part of chin. . . black hair. . . beautiful glossy shine on that hair. . . Oh man, I really need to touch up my own hair with some coloring. . . Oh god, I feel dull and unprepared. . . What am I doing here anyways? . . . WHO DO I THINK I AM??

What began as a simple complimentary thought about someone else turned into a comparison, and ultimately negative thoughts about themselves. This is why it's critical to STICK WITH THE FACTS when you are on step one.

Step 2. In – Bring your attention back to yourself (specifically on your body) and observe facts

Once you've established some facts around you and turned on that "observation mindset," then you can bring your attention inward. Bring your awareness onto yourself, specifically onto your body and the way it feels. Allow your awareness to drop into your physical body, noticing your breathing or where your body is attempting to draw your attention. Maybe you can feel your heart beating fast—if so, just observe that. Maybe the back of your neck feels sweaty, so simply observe the feeling of the moisture on your skin. Don't make up a story about it. Don't worry about it. Simply observe.

Once you've started observing your physical body, it's time to bring this awareness to the lower part of your body: your belly, your legs, your hips, your feet. Doing this helps to ground you. So much of your performance power is in your lower body, your connection with the earth, and the sexual energy at the base of your spine, so putting your attention here can have a calming and grounding effect.

A few ways to bring your attention to your lower body:

- Place your hand over your belly button and notice it move out and in as you breathe.

- Put your attention on your feet on the ground. Bend your knees slightly and imagine the entire bottom of your foot on the ground, toes spreading to embrace and support you standing there.

- Keeping your feet flat on the floor, gently shift your weight from one foot to the other, allowing your hips to shift and move as you do so.

- Place your hands firmly on your hips and squeeze your glutes (butt cheeks) one at a time.

Step 3. Out – Put your attention on the space or person around you, noticing what you "sense" or imagine about them

Now this time when you put your awareness outside of yourself, you're going to see what you can sense from the other person or the room around you. The best way to do this is to notice what first springs to mind. When you look at this person, what is your first thought about them? What do you sense they might be carrying with them, or the mood they're in? What do you imagine they are feeling right now? Perhaps you sense colors around them or emotions or attachments to another place—or perhaps you sense they are uncomfortable being looked at!

If you are putting your attention on a room, a theatre, or a space instead of one specific person, you might examine the energy in the room. Does it feel tense or relaxed? Are you sensing that the day has been dull and there's space for something new? Are the expectations high or are they low? Perhaps you're onstage, standing behind a curtain about to begin a show, and when you close your eyes and listen, you get the sense that the audience is rushed and a little tired. It's Friday night and there was traffic on the bridge, so you may be sensing the weariness of the work week and the urgency to get in their seats—the hurry up and relax of it all.

The important thing to remember is that this part of the exercise isn't about being right. Your intuitive sense may be highly developed and you may see something that is correct, or you may be projecting. It doesn't matter. The goal is to do your best to allow your awareness of this person or place to run deeper than what you can see with your eyes. The more you do this exercise, the more you will be able to drop into a place where you are right. But it is the reaching that counts at the beginning.

Step 4. In - Bring your awareness back onto your body and notice how it feels for you to receive this information from Step 3.

Now that you've sensed your partner or the space, bring that sensory awareness back into your own body and notice any emotions or feelings that arise from this new information. Say you just sensed that your partner is on edge or a little distracted. Notice how that feels in your body. Your shoulders may feel heavy, and you may sense a restlessness in your arms or a humming in your belly.

So often we observe or sense things in our environment, and then emotions arise out of this information—we are in a tense room and so we begin to feel tense, or we make up stories that people are mad at us or whatever—without ever observing this effect on us objectively. By bringing the awareness back onto your body, you are taking an objective look at the energy that this stirs, stimulates, or creates in your body so you have some navigational power over your own emotional movement.

In Step 4, we receive this sixth-sense type of information, feel it in our body, and begin to notice what wants to come forward. Back to sensing that your partner is on edge or distracted: you might feel your restless arms, do they want to reach out and give a hug to your partner? Your partner's shoulders, do they seem to be asking for your hands to press them gently down? Perhaps you feel the urge to simply keep your gaze connected with your partner while you smile with your eyes and wiggle your hips. As you stay focused on your own body receiving sensory information, you will begin to feel what is being called for in the moment— and you will find yourself inspired into action.

Step 5. Out - Gift the room, the audience, or your partner with inspired action

The fifth and final step is taking that received information and giving something to the moment. You probably do this all the time in performance without realizing it. Doing comedy in a bustling bar with people laughing and not paying attention may give you the inspired action to match that energy by saying your next joke louder or faster. Perhaps the room is a captive audience but they just need to be focused, and you sense that looking at them silently is just what they need. Whatever the action you are inspired to do, it is now more connected and more in-tune with the space. You've taken these few moments to tap into yourself and the room, and your gift of performance comes out of that connection.

I call this last step giving a gift for a reason. When you calm yourself down, pay close attention, and then meet the room where it is, you are truly a gift. What's better than a friend who gives you something that you're deeply desiring so much that you might not even be aware of it? There is nothing better. In this moment, you have made it less about you and more about them and you.

Wheel of Energy!

The reason I call this a watermill is not simply because a watermill brings water in and out but because of the watermill's basic function—to generate energy. That is the magic that happens when the Watermill is happening. When you're connecting to self, then connecting to an audience, then back again, an energy is created that surpasses the individual parts. The sum is greater than the whole!

As a quick reference, you can remember these steps like this:

Step 1. Out – SEE

Step 2. In – FEEL

Step 3. Out – SENSE

Step 4. In - REACT

Step 5. Out – GIFT

Why It Works

The Watermill works because you are doing the very thing that your nervous (fight or flight) system wants you to do—you are taking in the situation and tuning yourself to what's going on, much as you would have tuned yourself to a dangerous situation. You are then turning those physical symptoms into expressive action and giving somewhere for that nervous fear energy to go.

20 Ways to Connect With Your Audience On Stage and Off

Here are some practical things you can do to connect with your audience. As you begin to use them, notice which ones rely on tension-building and which utilize vulnerability. Sometimes, they might employ both. The more you understand what you're doing when you engage with your audience and your intentions behind your actions, the more likely you are to connect from an honest, heart-centered place. And the more you stretch yourself in using vulnerability and tension, you'll find your fear of the other dissolving as your confidence in being received well by your audience increases.

1. Don't wait to connect: Establishing connection with the audience is your first priority, so whatever else you've decided to do first—whether it's establishing a character, setting up the time/place, opening with something high-energy, etc.– it must be done with the intention of connecting with the crowd and eliciting their buy-in. Skip this step, and nothing else matters.

2. Do your research: Who is your audience? Are they young? Old? Of a specific gender? Aligned with certain political beliefs? If you don't know where to start finding this information, look no further than yourself. We often attract audience members who have many things in common with us. We might just present an aspirational version of themselves. Understanding who is in your fan base and what they might be dealing with in their own lives helps you in the articulation stages of creating and performing your work. If you know them, you'll have a better idea of how to curate the experience for them.

3. Create a shared "insider" world with references, call backs, and a cohesive universe: In *The Creative Formula*, I call this the "weird little rules of your universe." Everyone enjoys the experience of being "in the know" or part of a community (albeit temporary) that an audience can provide. Once you are clear on the landscape you are offering to the audience, then it becomes a playground that you invite your audience into. Establishing your style, tone, direction, developing your own language within it, all these things create the feeling of being in on the joke, or inside this special little world with you.

4. Give them your undivided attention . . . when you can: When you are supposed to be connecting with them at certain points then make sure that you really and truly are all there. It might be those first few moments when you first step onto the stage, after the show when you're greeting people in the lobby, or when you ask the audience a question and listen for a response. In all of these moments, do your best to be present, listen to what they have to say, pay attention to what's going on, and give them your full attention, even if it's only for a short period of time.

5. Be authentic: How do you show up authentically? You begin by getting honest about where you are when you begin a performance. Only when you're honest with where you've started do you have the power to shift it or journey somewhere else. The audience can sense when you're "trying too hard". Begin authentically, and then they'll be more likely to come with you and enjoy the ride.

6. Ask the audience a question or elicit audience engagement of some kind: When we're sitting in a dark theater or are simply on the audience side of a performance, it can be really easy to just check out and go into a passive mode . . . which can easily slip into a bored mode where we aren't paying attention. So, it's helpful, whenever possible, to find ways to make the audience participate. Can you introduce the show by asking them a question? Can they take part in some moment with applause or saying some words? Don't be afraid to ask something of them.

7. Take that in and respond: If you do ask them a question, then make sure you listen to the answer. If you ask them to do something, pay attention to how they're doing it. Sounds simple, but if you're requesting participation, it's really important that you cement that circle of trust by acknowledging they did what you asked of them.

8. Share food together: Ok, maybe this isn't always possible (or appropriate), but eating is an intimate act that as humans we've done in community for millenia. It can make people feel warm, fuzzy, nourished, sensual. It engages more of the senses: taste, smell, touch. When it makes sense, consider it.

9. Approach your presentation from your audience's perspective: This goes back to the very first tip. Who is in that crowd? How can you draw in their experience, their energy, and consider their needs? Without considering them, you risk the danger of allowing their experience of your performance to be distanced, objectifying, and voyeuristic. When you do consider them, you will naturally think of ways that allow for the experience to be more immersive, involved, and personalized.

10. Follow up with them afterwards: If you did your job right, chances are they are thinking about you the next day. But with so much content coming into our lives every day, their attention might not span much farther than that. Have an email ready to send to new audience members the next day asking them to connect with you on social media or, giving them another way to connect with you and your work. Follow up with them while you're hot on their minds.

11. Do what you say and say what you do: So much of trust building has to do with following through with your promises and delivering on what you said you would do—which really all boils down to integrity. So, it's a good idea to think of how you can tell them what you're going to do and then follow through on that promise. It's a clear indication that you're good on your word. My mind goes to Hannah Gadsby's comedy special, Douglas, where she starts off by telling you what she will say and do throughout the set and then she does it. She does this in such an explicit way that it becomes a well-conceived gag. But it doesn't always have to be executed this way. This same device can be employed in smaller more subtle ways as well.

12. Establish eye contact: When you have a show where there is no "fourth wall" (ie. You don't have to pretend the audience isn't there), it never hurts to make eye contact. The reason I think performers may avoid it is they can find it overwhelming, or they're afraid to see whatever they might find in an audience's eyes, be it admiration or judgement. My answer to this is twofold: First, you don't have to look at "all" the eyes, just pick one person to connect with at a time. Second, look for the eyes that are looking at you—in other words, those that are the most engaged and the most interested. Chances are you'll find only support in those gazes.

13. Try to identify what might be offensive or triggering and consider preparing your audience for that: If you're going somewhere jarring, then it's important to find a way to warn your audience, whether it's by directly telling them at the top of the show or having foreshadowing events or signs that lead up to it in a slow enough way that by the time it happens they're prepped for it, they know it's coming. Nothing breaks trust faster for an audience member than to be thrown into a traumatic state with no lead up.

14. If you have a program for your audience, use it to create connection, context, and credibility: While you shouldn't lean on your program to explain your show, you can include things that will help your audience connect more to the material, to you, or to your work in general. That's why many programs often include a note from the director (creating an "insider" familiarity), biographies (creating awe, excitement, and interest in the artists involved), and sometimes even answers to potential audience questions by including things like instructions on whether photography is allowed, intermission breaks, after-party invitations, etc. This is another way that you can both say what you're going to do and then follow through and do what you say.

15. Use storytelling: Have you ever watched something abstract and noticed that even though there isn't a story present, your mind will constantly be looking for clues to create a story to latch onto? Our brains are hardwired for story, so good artists use it whenever possible. When you offer the audience a story (no matter how vague or abstract or seemingly nonsensical), you are tacitly implying: We have a plan. We're going somewhere together. There will be a beginning, middle and an ending, and you may learn something.

16. Get personal: There is sometimes the misunderstanding that personal equals unprofessional, but this absolutely does not have to be the case. You are always choosing which details of something personal to share, so while it can feel vulnerable to get personal with your crowd, you can curate it in a way that allows you to do it without relinquishing your professionalism. Instead of thinking of getting personal as "messy," "unhinged," "reckless," think of it instead as "open," "provocative," "honest."

17. Don't be afraid of emotion: In addition to getting personal with your audience, you can also communicate from a place of emotion (as long as it's honest). Sometimes we can become so focused on what we are saying that we forget how or why we are saying it—which is the emotional connection that makes people care to begin with. The most evocative, connecting communication combines both the intellect and the emotions.

18. Use your body: We are viscerally connected creatures. Don't just stay up in your head—let what you're doing embody all of you. Have you ever watched a dancer move and found yourself inadvertently moving or jerking in response? Our bodies mirror each other, so the more you are embodied as a performer, the more you will light up the bodies of those watching you, creating a connection that runs deeper than the intellect.

19. Check in with your audience during the show: When you embark on your performance, be sure to look back every once in a while at your audience to make sure they're keeping up, need a break or are even still there. Don't just connect and take off. Connect back in again and again throughout your performance.

20. Use social media to connect before and afterwards: Like it or not, social media has become an essential part of the world we create as performers. It's the new waiting room, the new real-time peanut gallery, the new post-show lobby. Look at it not so much as a necessary evil, but as an added opportunity. It's just one more place to share intimate details of your creative process (adding to that "insider" feeling), to say what you're going to do (building that trust integrity), and to learn exactly who is in your audience and how they're receiving your work.

Your Mission, Should You Choose to Accept It: You have to start somewhere. Pick one of these twenty suggestions to try out this week. Next week, try a different one. Do this for four weeks and see how you feel. Do you feel more connected? Are you seeing a difference in engagement with your audience? In their response to you or your work? What's working for you that you could do more of? What's not working that you can let go of and stop doing to make space for better things?

Connecting With Yourself

There is one major block that can stand in the way of being able to manage your fear and connect with your audience—and that is being disinterested in yourself. If you're feeling lackluster, uninspired, or down on yourself, then chances are it isn't what you think. No, you are not boring! If you review your life a little ways back, you will likely discover that at some point you broke trust with yourself. We don't always recognize it as such, but when experienced, it can be one of the most painful heartbreaks we ever endure in life.

Breaking Your Own Heart

The first person we ever break trust with is ourselves. In those first moments in our life where we experience failure, shattered dreams, or shame, we find ourselves turning to self-doubt, regret, and self-hate. We leave (even if only temporarily) our spirit's alignment and we become mis-aligned, broken away from ourselves, and we flail with the uncomfortable feelings that arise from the split. We betray ourselves. We break our own hearts first. And then if that is never mended, others' betrayals (and our acceptance of them) follow easily. But let it be understood: the first fissure happens within.

Often when you have a hard time asking an audience to trust you, it is because at some point along the way, you have stopped trusting you. You've felt this split, this betrayal of self. Perhaps you broke a promise to yourself or you fell apart during an audition or a performance. Maybe you showed up for everyone else, but you neglected those things you want for yourself. Or maybe you've broken your heart by fumbling in your choices. You made a choice, but not wholeheartedly, and now you've begun to doubt yourself.

This is generally one of the first matters I have to address with the majority of the artists I coach: how to rebuild the trust that they've lost with themselves. Trusting yourself is the scaffolding for everything else to be built. Who wants to be led by someone who doesn't trust themselves to lead?

The most painful heartbreak is the disconnection from self.

Signs that You Don't Trust You

Jealousy of others' successes

Sinking feeling in your chest when you imagine going for something new

Increase in self-doubt

Feeling of wanting to give up

Knowing what you want but feeling immobilized to begin

Procrastination

Over-seeking of other people's opinions

Rebuilding Self-Trust

There is only one solution to getting back to feeling fully capable, and that is earning your trust back, just as you would with a friend or a loved one: one moment, one action at a time.

When it comes to rebuilding trust with self, I recommend going slowly. This could look like setting aside only fifteen minutes a day to create at first. Maybe for you this is writing, or sending emails to get a project rolling, or dancing, or practicing your set, your monologue, your piece in front of the mirror. And at the end of the week, it's about being happy with yourself if you managed to do those fifteen minutes 50% of the time. Next week try for all seven days, then slowly increase the amount of time you want to spend creating, practicing, or performing.

Try stacking this new fifteen-minute creative habit on top of something else that you do regularly so it follows a habit. For example, brush your teeth and then do your fifteen minutes. If you have a good gym habit, then go to the gym and then go straight to the studio or writing desk. Get your materials together and have them easily accessible. Decide where you're going to do your creative habit. Let others know that this is a time you are not to be disturbed. Set yourself up for success as much as possible.

Cut Out the Negative Self-Talk

All too often I hear artists talk about their laziness, procrastination, and flakiness to others almost like it's a badge of honor. It's often done as a way to sidestep a compliment. This irks me. I believe we learn to do it because we see it as a way of being humble. When we do this, we are taking care of others by soothing their own fears of not enough. But it isn't helpful for anyone. And if you're already feeling untrustworthy with yourself, it just reinforces the feeling.

Imagine if you had a child and people always pointed and said, "Oh, they're so smart!" And you responded with something like, "Oh, they're pitifully lazy! They could do so much more if they could just get their act together!" What a

Holly Shaw

terrible thing for a parent to say! I've heard plenty of stories of parents who do just that, but I see it as abuse. Plain and simple, bad mouthing yourself is abuse. So, notice when you're bad mouthing yourself to others and see if you can stop yourself before you do. The first step to forgiving yourself is to stop berating yourself to others.

At first it may feel awkward to simply say, "Thank you," when someone gives you a compliment. But with time, that muscle will grow and your inner creative child will feel more calm and supported and be given an environment to flourish without the squashing and bad mouthing.

Winning Yourself Back

What would it feel like to win yourself back? To romance yourself? Support yourself like the parent/partner/teacher you'd always wished you had? So much is possible when we put in the effort to rebuild trust within ourselves. And we can do it moment by moment, bit by bit. The goal is to find whatever slivers of stability you have and build on them.

Imagine if someone else broke your heart: you'd be pissed! You'd have the option to just walk away from that person if you really wanted to. But the kicker here is that you are stuck with you. You can't just walk away from yourself. But you are also capable of abandoning yourself on an emotional level, which causes a split in your soul: there's the higher part of you that loves you and will never leave you, but in your actions, words, and beliefs, you've given up on yourself. Two parts of you are stretching in different directions, and this is what causes the pain inside.

Imagine mending this trust just like you would with anyone else. You're giving yourself major side eye, so it isn't the time to try to make big romantic gestures. Don't make big flashy promises that you can't follow through with. Think of it as courting yourself. How much do you trust a lover that seduces you as soon as you meet them? Or one who breaks your heart, but then appears on your doorstep proclaiming love the next day? That's tough to trust. You would be suspicious of that behavior. So, don't try to rebuild self-trust with empty, far-reaching promises.

Show up. Do what you say. Say what you do. Show yourself affection consistently. Be generous with yourself. And also, give yourself space if you're still not ready to fully trust. Have faith and go slowly with small, consistent actions.

Your Love & Fear Elixir: Where and when have you broken your own heart? How did you mend that rift? What helped you moved past that experience and into a more loving place?

Connecting: You See? You Already Know How to Do This

When we're thrown in the middle of madness one day, and then the next, and then the next, it scatters us. Gives us the predominant sensation that we are never in the right place. That there's something more important we should be paying attention to. It disconnects us. We might feel as though we're floating through time, suspended or frozen.

> **The chaos can hurl us into doubt, fear, and anxiety, all of which leaves us unsure what to do next.**

But as artists, this isn't something that we haven't faced before. In fact, we have encountered it many times.

Have you ever been brought to a dead stop in the middle of an audition because your mind has drawn a complete blank? Or found yourself coming up short in front of a crowd during a performance? It can feel like the rug has been pulled out from underneath you! It can derail the trajectory of your entire performance—if you let it. But if you've managed to power through these situations, it's likely because you were able to use the attributes of Connection—tension, vulnerability, and trust—in some combination in order to navigate your way through it.

What's Happening When We Choke

When you come up blank on a line, forget where you're headed, or lose your place, it's simply because a connection was broken—a distraction from the present moment, a disconnection from the audience, or a disconnection from your self (which is typically a negative or self-critical thought). And so, it can only be through connection that we've been able to make our way through these troubling situations.

I had this happen to me once when I was teaching a workshop at SAG/ AFTRA Headquarters in L.A. I was speaking to a room full of 120 professional actors. Things were going well. The actors in the audience were engaged. I was fully engaged in my content and I began a very passionate sentence and then . . .

for whatever reason . . . my mind went blank. Now, I have been here many times in my life. And I know by now that in those moments, we all have a clear choice:

> You can disconnect from the audience and freak out. . . or you can stay connected, accept what's happening, and wait for something to come to mind.

So, here's what happened next:

I allowed the Tension to grow:

I paused. The room paused with me. The tension mounted as they waited to hear how that oh-so-passionate sentence was going to end. Oh boy! The pressure was ON!!!

So, then I turned to Vulnerability:

After a moment or two of looking around the room, I realized the thought was not going to return to me, and so I simply looked at everyone and said, "I just completely drew a blank." That's it. I just admitted it. Not with an apology. But just as an admittance of where I was. I let myself be vulnerable and share what was really going on with me and, more importantly, I maintained connection with the room and the present moment.

And finally, I leaned on the Trust that I had already built with them:

Up until that point in the seminar, things had been going great, so I gave myself the benefit of the doubt. I not only trusted in myself that I'd figure out what to do next, but I also trusted that they would stay with me if I was just honest. The result was that they laughed. And once the tension in the room broke with that laughter, I finally remembered what I had wanted to say next and we moved on.

Now, I know that during an audition, you don't always have the option to break character and say, "I forgot the line." but you do have a choice: You can FREAK OUT, make yourself wrong, and break your connection to the character, the room, and your scene partner, thereby making everyone uncomfortable . . . or you can ACCEPT what's happening and therefore stay connected to the room, to the moment, and allow yourself the time to see what's going to come to you.

Every time you've managed to recover from choking on stage it is for the simple reason that you said 'yes' to it. You've found a way to be ok with it. If you had a partner, maybe you looked at them and taken a cue from them.

You stayed connected. To yourself. To the moment. And to the people in the room.

In this same way, you will get through these disconnected times. This time. And the next and the next. Soon, you will develop deep trust in yourself.

We can't always be perfect, and we can't always control conditions or experiences, but we can make the most of them. When that fear arises, we can learn how to utilize it and transform it into something better.

When you don't know what to do next,
when you feel frozen, lost or uninspired, try connection.
It's something you've known how to do all along.

Part II

Dealing with the Fear of Not Enough

Fear of Not Enough

Also Known As: Fear of failure, fear of poverty, fear of missed opportunity, fear of regret

Mindset: Scarcity

Shadow Self: The Rebel

Adrenaline Response: Fight

Mode of Operation: Limitation

Key for Evolution: Giving and receiving freely, enjoying reaching without measuring yourself against the crowd

Limiting Belief: "There's not enough (time, space, resources) to go around."

Manifests As: Playing it small, shrinking, or the opposite, stealing the scene, being a show hog, grabbing for more than what's needed, obsessive, comparison of self to others

New Belief: "The world is abundant and infinite in its resources."

Trust In: There is enough

Connect With: Abundant universe, people that see your worth, activities that make you feel good

Create: Opportunities for receiving

New Story: "There's plenty to go around and enough for everyone."

Repeat Daily: "I have everything I need."

Marissa calls me up in a panic. She just came from an audition where it didn't go so hot. She confesses that she may have psyched herself out. "I was feeling pretty good when I got there," she tells me. "I had prepared pretty well, but then I walk into the waiting room and there is . . ." She pauses and sighs dramatically. "No joke, about thirty girls that look just like me, only way prettier and thinner. Ugh! I know I shouldn't worry about that, but I couldn't help but thinking about how there's so many of us, and so alike. Who am I to think I'm going to be the one they pick? By the time I got called in to audition twenty minutes later, I was just feeling so full of doubt, and so frustrated too! So many of my friends have been booking things and . . . well, when am I going to book anything?? Maybe there's just too many people with my same look here in L.A.

It's not an unfamiliar sentiment. There are a lot of potential actors, and often more of them aren't working than those who are. You can definitely point to evidence supporting this belief that there aren't enough jobs to go around.

And yet, remember that we aren't arguing against the need for this fear or the validity of having it—we are attempting to replace it with a belief that is more helpful.

The fear of not enough is one of the most powerful of all fears because it's been conditioned into us that we are limited. When we don't want to finish our dinners as children, we are told that "there are starving children in Africa." We have and they do not. And if we could only be less selfish, then others could have more. This belief is often holed up behind the mask of generosity and selflessness: We should have less so others can have more. We're taught that this is kindness and that wanting more or expanding is somehow selfish, greedy, or grabby.

But I would argue that selfishness actually comes directly from this belief of not enough. When we are afraid that our needs won't be met, that's when we stockpile more than we need for the future. When we are worried that we won't shine compared to someone else, then that's when we "steal the scene" or play outside the rules to get our few minutes in the spotlight.

But when we live from the belief that the universe is abundant, that there's enough for all, a funny thing happens:

We relax, we exhale. We smile and we feel generous. Because the need to "grab ours" has vanished. There's no need to grab for a tiny piece when we realize that there's an infinite amount available whenever we'd like to reach for it. There's no need to regret an opportunity that has passed when we recognize that there are always more opportunities coming.

Indicators of Fear of Not Enough

Shrinking or Playing it Small

One common way to deal with the fear of not enough is to shrink or play it small. When we do this, it's a sign that at some point we've been trained out of feeling our innate worthiness. When we've been shown or taught that we will always be seen or received in a certain way no matter what we do, we may start to believe that there is no reason to try. We can settle. We can stay right where we are, play it like we know how, take less risks, and try to be happy with our little piece of the pie.

But we are not built to settle. We, just like the little Hobbit from The Lord of the Rings, seek comfort but we also seek adventure, risk, and travel. And so, a disconnect is created between what we think we want and what we deeply crave. That is what happens when we play it small and safe.

Here's something important to remember: Not everyone is going to want to "be a star," and not everyone has the same desire to "play big!" We all have different markers of what it means to excel, and that's glorious! It's also exactly why this fear is unsubstantiated—we often have the fear of not enough because of the unfounded belief that everyone wants the same exact thing. (News flash: they don't!)

Playing it small means different things for different people. This isn't about reaching for an idea or version of yourself that you "think" you should be striving for. It's about striving for what truly nourishes your spirit. And only you can know what that looks like.

When you reach for something really high, you don't always meet your goal—but you can be left with the sense of satisfaction for having stretched yourself into a bigger shape. Reaching isn't always about getting. It's about the growth inside you that happens in the attempt.

Resignation

But this other thing can happen where you let yourself feel like a failure. You feel like because you didn't meet the benchmark that you set for yourself, then you may as well have not tried at all.

When we play it small, there is a resignation of spirit that sets in. A sadness begins to creep in when we put the brakes on our own momentum. All of a sudden, things and people around you appear to be moving faster as you shake your head and expend more energy than you'd like because you're digging your heels in.

Frustration

After resignation follows waves of frustration. Frustration is the emotion that arises when we try to stay small and safe. Frustration comes no doubt from our deeper craving for movement. We are always moving towards something, and if we try to stop that movement, we'll feel a deep frustration. Our soul wants to move, but we are in the way. Our spirit says "fly!" And we say, "No! Stay safe!" It's a mis-alignment, and it creates frustration. Imagine that you are your own parent urging your inner child to go to college and yet they just want to live at home and play video games. Oh, the frustration! This is the same thing you're doing to yourself when you try to "stay put."

Self-Doubt

In order to alleviate the pain of frustration, we give into self-doubt. When you resign yourself to non-movement, you're re-confirming and feeding into your self-doubt. You're telling yourself to stay safe, and through inaction, you are confirming your fear of not being good enough. It actually helps you feel a little bit better to convince yourself that you were right to stay put. The problem is, playing small creates a self-fulfilling prophecy that you don't deserve more. Eventually it's easy to look around and find evidence for your self-doubt and your resignation. You say to yourself, "Well, I've not done anything more, so therefore I don't deserve anything more."

Bitterness and Jealousy

When you've decided to settle for less than your creative spirit longs for, you begin to resent others that haven't settled. You find yourself thinking negative or critical thoughts about those around you—perhaps even distaste—because you can't find joy for them without feeling disappointment in yourself. You feel the opposite of generous and loving, and it's this tightness of being that is most painful. Thankfully, it can often be the wakeup call for people to change something in their lives and stop letting this fear of not enough rule them.

Show Hog, Stealing the Scene

Another common way the fear of not enough shows up is the opposite of playing small, which is doing things to steal the scene or draw attention. This shouldn't be confused with shining full out. If you are feeling great onstage or in life, then please please please, by all means shine shine SHINE ON! When your shine comes from a place of feeling deeply confident in yourself and in love with the world, then this can inspire others to do the same.

Instead, I'm talking about the scene stealing that comes from desperation or worry that you won't be seen. People always talk about stealing the show like it's a good thing, but when I hear those words, I think of people who consciously upstage you. Hogging the stage or upstaging someone is very different from playing to your full potential or really shining fully onstage. What I'm talking about are those times when someone switches the rules on you.

We've all experienced this at some point or another, and it's a total nightmare. I remember working with dancers who would change the choreography onstage. We may have rehearsed it a hundred time, but once they hit the stage, they'd do something totally different that would make me go "Whaaaaaat?" Or the artist who messes up, and when the audience laughs, they decide to lean into it and to improv and make it all about them gratuitously. Or the musician who doesn't play full out in rehearsal, but then does several upstaging things during the show that throws everyone off. Everyone's like, "what's happening now?" Or my personal favorite, the dancer who decides to do a piece and they just leave you alone onstage. There you are, fake grin plastered on your face, wondering "Where the hell did they go?" It's a total nightmare that leaves the other people onstage scrambling to catch up.

All of these things have happened to me in professional settings, and I'm sure if you've spent any length of time working onstage with others, you can relate to some of these situations as well.

What's so unfair about this sort of thing is that it breaks trust and damages the integrity of the entire performance.

Competitiveness

When someone begins to act out of this fear of not enough, it makes others start to wonder if there's a shortage and they begin to grab too. It can spark an unhealthy competitiveness in everyone involved. Instead of being invested in the whole production or project going well, people begin to narrow their concern to themselves.

I've seen directors actually create a competitive atmosphere among dancers in order to (supposedly) elicit their best from people, but in reality, it has very little short-term gain. Using competitiveness to push people to their full potential has the opposite effect in the long run.

Greediness

While people may work a little harder at first to win the approval of the director, eventually the competitiveness leaves people greedy and looking out only for themselves. The worst part about greediness is it robs you of the joy of being generous. It stops the flow of giving and receiving energy. Just as a heart beats, bringing blood into it and pumping it back out, so too you are designed to not only receive but also to give. Greediness stops the flow of blood. You take yourself out of the wheel of abundance. You get "backed up," so to speak, and so begin to receive less and less.

Secretiveness, Manipulating, Blaming, and Shaming

Pretty much everyone understands that "greediness" is not an attractive look, so instead of living honestly, you become secretive in order to sustain your greediness. You may even try to divert attention away from yourself and onto someone else. Manipulating, blaming, shaming other people. All of the work it takes to maintain your greediness can weigh heavily on you, creating intense pressure. A way to alleviate some of the stress of this, even if only briefly, is pointing the finger somewhere or to someone else.

Biting Off More Than You Can Chew (aka Stockpiling)

Another way that fear of not enough can show up is in over-committing to things. Maybe your competitiveness and greediness shows up not in comparison to other people, but with yourself. It's more of a stockpiling situation. Checklists, goals, and accomplishments become not just a structure to help you create but shackles keeping you on task. The thinking is, "Well, I should take every opportunity I have because I don't know when I might have another one." This mindset says that you have to make it to the finish line first, but all that does is put unnecessary pressure on yourself.

Feeling Like You're Not "Enough"

The result of stockpiling is that it can eventually create an overall feeling that you are not enough. Maybe you didn't start out that way, but eventually, all these "overdoing" actions leave you with the sense that you are only as good as your next great work. Productivity becomes the only measuring stick.

I can't help but think about New Year's resolutions. Every year, around November or December, I take about a week off to really reflect on what I accomplished and how I lived the past year. I take time to brainstorm what things I might like to create in the coming year. The problem with this is that I often would over commit myself at the beginning of the year to creating more than is healthy, and by October, I find myself burnt out and disgruntled I hadn't advanced farther. I wasn't living my best life.

Nowadays, I'm becoming more careful about biting off more I can chew. As much as I want to create things—write new books, perform, etc.—I also want to live a good, healthy, balanced life. I want to have time to reflect and make creative pivots in my plans—not just at the end of the year, but all throughout. I want to play and rest and see friends for no productive or work-related reason, but simply to relax and have fun.

Now, with this new resolution, I've found the emotions that arise sometimes are uncomfortable feelings of not enough. There are times that I have a nagging feeling that I'm not doing enough, but it's been important for me to see that for what it is—the big fear of not having "enough." I know that in reality, life has many creative ideas and opportunities awaiting me, and maybe, just maybe, I'll do even better with them. I'll certainly enjoy them more when I'm not rushing to finish them all at once!

Living in the Past

Another result of feeling like there isn't enough is that you can get stuck in rehashing and reminiscing about the past. The thinking goes, "There isn't hope now, but oh boy, remember the good old days?" It's a things were better when mentality, and it's costly because it gives all your power away to something that's finished instead of investing in what's happening right now.

There's a funny phenomenon about remembering the past: When you become nostalgic for your past successes, you often forget that at the time of that success you were actually reaching even higher! The success that you're nostalgic for might have actually felt like a failure at the time. You are hungry for a ghost of a happier self that never even existed.

Regret

Living in the past gives way to regret. Not only are you not enough now, but it turns out that you never were! You pass judgement on your past self, convincing yourself that you never were enough—never brave enough, dedicated enough, committed enough. This leads to a deep sense of regret and with that shame. A shame that can only be healed through forgiveness of yourself, but guess what? You don't feel like you deserve forgiveness, and so you resign yourself to a cycle of regret and resignation that keeps you planted solidly where you are—stuck, creatively blocked, and blinded by your own self-criticism.

As you can see the fear of not enough can fast track you into a downward spiral of despair and stuckness. But that's where another one of your shadow selves steps in.

This next one has a ton of energy for what they lack in discretion and that keeps you on your toes.

Wanting to protect you from embarrassment, mediocrity, or overwork, it will swoop in to admonish what others think before you care too much or encourage you to skip school. When called upon for accountability though, it will place the blame anywhere else in order to maintain its viewpoint.

It gives no fucks. Meet the Rebel.

Signs That You Are Allowing
The Fear of Not Enough to Run You

You are always keeping track: what you've got, who has what, what's going on in comparison to you. When opportunities arise, you feel an urgency to jump on it that feels unhealthy or throws you off balance. You compare yourself to others. You call attention to yourself often. You feel rushed or like time is running out. You ask yourself, "Who do I think I am?" In your mind, you are living often in the past. You manipulate situations to remain "on top." It matters greatly to you how others see you. You feel complacent and reluctant to change.

Your Shadow Self: The Rebel

The shadow self that arises out of the fear of not enough is the Rebel.

When I was on that plane and started making noises like I was riding a roller-coaster, that was the Rebel taking charge: throwing a little fun and mockery to ease the tension of a tough situation. That was the Rebel at their best. At their worst, the Rebel might make fun of the person crying next to them, play a trick on a scared person to exacerbate their fear, or simply plug in their earbuds and sing obnoxiously while the plane is tumbling.

At their best, the Rebel is someone who throws the rules out the window to inject playfulness into a situation. They love challenging authority and the status quo in an effort to seek justice. The Rebel is slippery to pin down; they may flip flop between sides or their positions on something. Either way, they love an extreme and pushing against something. They're usually saying 'hell no!' They're either flipping off the entire group as they sashay away or they're at the helm leading an angry mob.

At their worst, this shadow self manifests as total menace, refusing to do their homework while throwing pencils at other students instead, criticizing those kids who do care, mocking the committed, and flouting the norm.

As young artists, at some point we had to access our Inner Rebel in order to challenge the status quo and become who we were meant to be. Being able to argue your way out of doing things that are mundane, chore-like tasks can be beneficial to creating newer and better systems, but they can also get in the way of getting anything accomplished. When we're in the weeds or get overwhelmed with a project, we access the Rebel in order to lighten up, switch the script, blow off steam, and take a break.

The Rebel gives themselves license to not care, to resist forward progress, and to completely change direction in an effort to take the pressure off themselves. They love throwing a wrench in the momentum by using tools such as apathy and criticism (of self and of others). What can be freeing and liberating in the right contexts can also be a source of chaos and self-destruction when taken too far. And eventually frustration. An overused Rebel secretly knows that they are their own

"Creativity is the greatest rebellion in existence."

– Osho

worst enemy and becomes frustrated with their own apparent lack of being able to settle down and simply get things done.

The Rebel likes to pretend to be on the outskirts, but unlike the Outlaw, they are more likely to find themselves with a following. Their emphatic opinions and not-a-care-in-the-world attitude has a kind of cool kid appeal even though underneath lies a deep well of discontent and self-doubt. Even though they pretend to be above it (or even part of solving it), the Rebel loves drama, gossip, and enticing others to play hooky with them. And they love keeping score. In this way, they are stuck in the past.

The Rebel lives anywhere but in the present. When it comes to the past, they are resentful, and when the future is concerned, they are reluctant and non-committal. When faced with a deadline, your Rebel says, "Forget this! I'm going to avoid creating, I'm never settling down or focusing on any one thing." The Rebel almost seems like they don't want to be happy because the struggle is more fun. But they still want points for their misery.

Creating a wake of unfinished projects and unfulfilled promises behind them, they eventually exhaust people in their relentless fun-seeking. They go wide, not deep. They scatter themselves far and then complain that they don't have enough time, resources, or energy to make good on their promises. Giving the appearance of creativity, they are only as brilliant as their next shiny idea. And the more they leave unfinished, the more deeply they sink into not trusting that they'll ever be worthwhile at all. They fear they are not enough and therefore they pretend not to care in the first place. They know the moment that they actually commit and finish something, they might be faced with the reality that the result isn't so great after all. They use perfectionism as an excuse to never finish.

"The only people who ever called me a rebel were people who wanted me to do what they wanted."

– Nick Nolte

"Being rebellious has two ways . . . One is simply standing against tyranny and injustice which is the world's collective way. You have nothing to lose other than your voice which is a very big thing. And the other is being a rebel to your close ones, for they do believe in you but they doubt the path you've chosen, the risk you're taking. And this rebellion is the hardest. To resist the shadow of care willingly and at the same walking together with them and here you can lose yourself."

- The Rhymester

Holly Shaw

Appeasing The Rebel:	The Rebel has to be willing to listen to people who are starkly honest with them—so long as they are ultimately on their side. The Rebel has a lot of raw energy that can be channeled back into creativity. They just need guidance and accountability. Their ability to fight, trust their instincts, rebel against authority, and cross boundaries can make them a powerful ally in creation. When accessed properly, the Rebel creates a thrilling diversion and can inject the humdrum with a spark of inspiration once again.
Important to The Rebel:	Drama, being the exception, keeping track,fairness, justice.
How The Rebel Handles Fear:	With stoicism, their strength is their connection to self; by fleeing, where they try to outrun their pursuer; occasionally in a stand-off but they're more likely to dodge a bullet or disappear when your back is turned than they are to actually fight.
Admired for:	One of two extremes: either head-on in a fiery rage,or total avoidance.
The Rebel says:	"Whatever!" or simply "No."
Famous Rebels:	James Dean (Rebel Without A Cause), Harriet Tubman, Joan of Arc, Madonna

Creativity: Exploring Your Abundance

When it comes to dealing with the fear of not enough, creativity, in all its abundance and flow is where we can find a remedy.

In this context, I'm using the word, "creativity" to mean being flexible, present in the moment, open to changes in direction, ability to play the game in front of you, and being open to new ideas and new ways of working. All of these things are more important than ever in times of distress and avalanches of madness. In other words, the free-flowing creative state of mind.

Even though creativity is supposedly number one on our daily "to do" list, we still have to remind ourselves to stay limber. As artists, creativity is our job, which is why it's so interesting that we're occasionally bad at it.

We sometimes have this notion that once a piece is created, there should be no creativity in the performance. Or we get lazy with it. This is a destructive way to think of a performance run. Creativity doesn't end once the choreography is set, or once the part is written. No matter how set in stone the notes, the script, the score, the jokes . . . creativity should infiltrate every performance. It is the sense that you are still alive up there. That you are connected, that you are responding to the moment, that you are willing to play with the chemistry of the room.

And creativity serves as an antidote to fear because it forces our inner perfectionist to take a rest. Our fear wants to tell us:

We have to keep a tight grip on everything otherwise who knows if it will turn out good enough

But these fears cannot exist inside a creative mind. As I've said many times,

Creativity is moving towards something, not away from it.

When you are interested, exploring, creating in the moment, you are moving towards something. But when you are afraid, you are pushing against your interest

When you're in a state of fear, your mind is running through worst-case scenarios and you are stuck in what you don't want. When you let go of there being one idea of perfection, you are allowing the best version (in that moment and for that audience) to rise to the surface. If you're constantly open to the moment creating itself, then you don't have one set idea of how it's all supposed to turn out. Once you're in a creative and allowing state of mind, then your thoughts are more productive:

I'm not sure where this is going, but I like it! And I know that there's plenty more ahead.

Huh, that's new and interesting!

Let's see exactly how this unfolds. . .

Example

Say you're writing a comedy and I give you the prompt of "What are 10 Reasons Your Ex and You Shouldn't Get Back Together," and the first thing you write is "#1 Because I'm a loser." But then you immediately say to yourself, "Ah, that's such a dumb idea! I don't want to get up in front of people and say that!" Then you have turned your back on the creative flow and stopped any momentum of ideas at all.

You're saying 'no' to your very first idea. You're moving away from something. That moving away is non-creative. It's a road to nowhere. Instead of saying 'no' to that, you must find a way to embrace it, use it as a toe hold to keep going it and find more.

Here's an example of how you can take an idea that at first doesn't seem great, but then you say 'yes' just to see where it goes:

"#1 I'm a loser . . . Ok, so . . . I'm a loser because, why? (I didn't say it was a crummy idea, only that it wasn't the end of the road). How can I flesh that out? What are some more details of that? What constitutes a 'loser?' I'm a loser because I wear sweatpants. I'm a sweatpants-wearing loser . . . " Then all of a sudden there's so many directions you go and you're just following the most interesting one. You're saying 'yes' and it's moving you forward to other and more ideas.

The inner critic is determined to stop the creativity from flowing, and all we want to do is to keep that creativity flowing. So, saying 'yes' to your ideas, no matter how crummy, helps you move on from them.

"*Every performance becomes a challenge, a new adventure of playing as if for the first time instead of a repetition of the night before. I can honestly claim that I will be more alive on stage at the end of a year's run than I was at the beginning.*"

– Uta Hagen

Training Yourself Into a "Yes" State of Mind

So, if creativity is always moving towards something, then what can we do in order to keep ourselves moving and not get stuck or resistant? We can learn to say "yes."

If I asked you to stop thinking negative thoughts, then guess where your attention goes? It goes straight to your negative thoughts. To truly train our minds into a creatively allowing state, I've got to give you an alternative, right? To stop amplifying the negative voices, you must have somewhere to put your attention—somewhere other than those negative thoughts. You have to find things to say "yes" to.

Saying "yes" is a muscle that gets stronger the more you exercise it. It's easy to look out into a world that's full of adversity and find nothing you want to say "yes" to, and so it takes focus. Here are some ways you can start training that "yes" muscle: by using it in your artistic life you will begin to also integrate into your everyday life.

Six Ways You Begin Training Your "Yes" Mind Today

1. Join An Improv Class or Group. Improvisational forms of theater have begun to really gain popularity over the last twenty years, and I think this is because people appreciate how improv develops a more creatively flexible mind. You are forced to be in the moment, saying "yes" to whatever your scene partners are doing. This makes you more solution-oriented, more flexible, and able to "go with the flow" in life in general.

2. Start Saying "Yes" in Rehearsals. If you have any control whatsoever over starting or stopping a scene, then stop stopping yourself whenever you make the tiniest mistake. See if you can flow through when you encounter a blip. Roll on with it—or even better, make it a new and interesting part of the rehearsal. Afterward, you can decide whether to incorporate it in the show or the pieces, or you can discard it—but in that moment, just go for it. I remember in high school theater, my director used to do one run of the show where she would purposefully create disasters—secretly telling an actor not to come on when they were supposed to, switching up the music, having the wrong set design come on at the wrong time, and so on. We had to figure out how to perform through or improvise around. It always created chaos and laughter, but it taught us to be flexible and ready for anything.

3. Practice "Yes" In the Studio. Are you lost on a project you've been working on and feeling like you would like to throw the whole project in the toilet? Instead of giving up, ask yourself, What can I say 'yes' to? or What is interesting to me right now? And then for the time being, set aside those other things you aren't sure about. Put a pause on the big picture and work only on that part that you can say "yes" to.

4. Say "Yes" to What You Eat. As you are going through the grocery store, give yourself a little extra time to pick up each item and before putting it in your cart. Ask yourself, Is this a 'yes'? Wait to see if you feel or think, yes! Notice how your body feels when you hold the different items. You might be surprised to find that things that you thought you were craving are actually a hmmm, nope, or even things you thought were healthy options, your body isn't saying yes to. This is a fun exercise because it's a basic human task—gathering one's food—and so it doesn't hold all the baggage that trying to apply yes to your rehearsals or performance might hold.

5. Look for Only "Yes" Before You Step Onstage. The time before a performance is a sacred time for me. From the moment of my call time to seconds leading up to the performance, I am dropping in and letting go of any outside conflicts—or even problems with the performance itself. I'm getting into a refined and high vibration state of being where I can be my optimum, creative self. When I'm producing or directing or part of a cast or group, I like to get everybody together before the show and do a little pre-show talk. I always end with telling everybody to begin saying yes and to not stop until they walk off the stage after the curtain call. This is a great practice to get into a creative mindset before a performance. I ask them to look around and say yes to everything that they can—look at the set and say yes. Their costume, Oh yes! Their castmates, Yes! I encourage them to be in that space of appreciation of everything they are interacting with before the show. Get yourself into a state of yes beforehand and you'll be amazed how problems tend to work out or turn into gold.

6. Have more conversations. We don't normally think of everyday conversations as improvisation, but they always are! The problem is that when we have conversations with people we are close to, we can sadly sometimes not listen as well as we could. We fall into patterns, we either hear what we want to hear, or we stop responding from an in the moment place. The good news is that we can unlearn these tendencies, and one way is to have conversations with other people— the grocery store checkout person, your fellow students in class, your next-door neighbor. When we begin to look at other people with interest and start engaging in conversation, we are training ourselves to be in the present moment, to listen, and to follow creativity.

Your Mission, Should You Choose to Accept It: Pick one of these to try this month. Commit to it. Have something to remind yourself to do it every day. See how you feel after the month. Are you feeling more relaxed or in tune with yourself?

The Rebel wants to make excuses for why you should say 'no'. They'll argue for their limitations, drag their feet and criticize the whole process if you let them.

An Artist's Incantation:

Before Walking Onstage Say "Yes"

Whatever you do

From now until you walk onto that stage

Whatever you do, say "yes"

Look at yourself in your costume, say "yes"

Warm up your body, say "yes"

Say "yes" to anything that is offered to you

Nod your head in appreciation when anyone says anything

Say "yes" to a hug

Say "yes" to everything right now

If you absolutely cannot say "yes"

Then just smile at the person kindly and

Simply turn and walk away

Start practicing "yes" right now

Because when you get on that stage

Everything must be "yes"

Whatever your partner does is a "yes"

Whatever you do is a "yes"

If you screw up, fall on the floor, vomit—it's a "yes"

Don't worry about something not going the way you planned

Because I can assure you, it will

Something will go wrong

And you will say "yes"

Because you know that in that moment

You are more present than you could have ever been

In an execution that was perfect

Your mistakes are your most honest moments

They are when the audience gets to see themselves in you

And you are their hero

So say "yes" to them

Say "yes" to your audience's belief in you

Say "yes" to yourself

"Yes" to your body

"Yes" to the people in the audience

To the people on stage sharing this with you, "Yes"

To the music, "Yes, yes"

I am

We are

Yes

Yes

Yes!

Falling In Love with The Voice In Your Head
. . . The Good One

So, what is keeping us from being creative in the moment? Perfection and all the ugly mean thoughts that we think about ourselves when we don't achieve it. The critical voices that weigh in with their woulda shoulda coulda perspectives. It's the false stories that have been projected onto us by others, our inner critic, our gremlins, our inner rebel kicking up dust and obscuring the clear view of who we really are.

Throughout our lives, we pick up different voices that we carry around in our heads. We are faced with a challenging situation, and we think of things our parents, teachers, siblings, friends, and lovers may have said about the situation. We see it through the eyes of many voices, and sometimes, they aren't positive. We're conditioned throughout our life to listen to this advice from others and seek counsel outside of ourselves. But the truth is, all of us have another voice that is solely our own that lives inside of us. It is guiding, positive, and says things like:

Oh yeah, I can do this.

Hey, I have an idea that I think will work.

Yeah, this feels right.

This is fun!

Our job as performers and creators is to fall in love with this voice in our head. The loving one. We need to listen to it until it speaks to us more frequently. We need to amplify it, give it a platform, and hush the noisy chatter of the other voices. We need to be willing to take a stand for it like any good ally might by shouting: Hey everyone, quiet down! I think my loving voice has something they would like to say!

You don't need to get rid of the other voices in your head. Those other voices may be trying to protect you. But we only want to make sure the loving voice is heard more often than not. We can take different perspectives into account (diversity only makes us better!), but we must create a safe space for the loving creativity inside of us to grow and bloom.

"We are rebels with a cause, poets with a dream, and we won't let this world die without a fight."

\- Albert Camus

It takes a bit of training. It takes noticing when you're going negative or beating yourself up and being willing to drop it. But just like when you are getting into a fight with a loved one, the energy and momentum can feel really monumental and hard to stop. You want to continue shouting at yourself and beating your fist in indignation when things don't go your way. But you can take a deep breath and decide the fighting isn't worth it. You can decide to let it go.

The beautiful thing about falling in love with this good voice in your head is that it's the very same voice that gives you the best creative ideas. And better yet, it responds well to attention. With your focus and practice to hearing it, it gets louder. The more you listen, the more it speaks to you, the more you'll hear, and the more ideas will come your way.

Your Love & Fear Elixir: What does your own good voice sound like? When you're in a flowing, creative state of mind, what kinds of things do you say to yourself? What does it feel like to hear these things? If this voice had a name, what would it be? If the voice was an actual voice (meaning it made a sound), what would that voice sound like? Raspy, like a jazz singer? Soft and sweet like a young mother singing to her baby? Deep and resonating like a warm father figure?

Play the Game

Every now and then I'll go to a baseball game, and I'll notice that, even when it is a Tuesday afternoon at 1 pm, you can find thousands of people sitting in the stands. It always baffled and disturbed me a bit. "Why," I would wonder, "are they able to get thousands of people to come to a baseball game on a Tuesday afternoon, but theaters sometimes struggle to get hundreds to come to their performance run on a Saturday night?" But instead of getting angry about this, I got curious. I realized that while there are probably a few reasons why this is so, there was definitely one big glaring explanation when I ask the question, "What makes baseball so damn riveting?"

The answer is in the creativity of the game itself. When a baseball player goes to bat, they don't pretend to hit the ball. They aren't trying to hit it like they did yesterday. They aren't trying to think of their character's qualities or history or background before they go to bat. They aren't thinking about how they look to the people in the stands when they hit that ball. They aren't worried about all these extra things. They are simply playing the game as it presents itself in that unique moment.

All the muscle, focus, and intention are focused one thing and only one thing. They are watching, in that moment, to see how the pitcher pitches that ball and doing everything they can in those passing milliseconds to hit it out of the park. Or they might decide in a split-second it's not worth it and they jump away from the pitch. But my point is, whatever they do, they have no time to worry about anything but playing that moment.

They aren't thinking about how the pitcher has pitched it in the past. They aren't thinking about how the audience in stands would like them to hit. They are wholly in the moment, creating that hit in a split-second to be as accurate and as powerful as possible. It's clear exactly what the stakes are. It's clear what the goal is. And all they are doing is trying to achieve that goal. And that kind of creative, singular focus is fascinating to watch.

All too often we concern ourselves with what other people think of us. We wonder if we are interesting enough, and yet, to be truly interesting is to be passionate about yourself. There's no need to worry about what others think—we can't control that anyhow! But what do YOU think? What are you interested in?

Performers have a lot they can learn from that kind of focus and that kind of creativity. You can't worry how it was yesterday. And you can't even worry too much over how you would like it to be today. You have to play the game in front of you. You have to be creative in the moment and work with what you've got. Not only will you be fascinating to watch if you do this, but the result could be even better than you could have dreamed.

"To Be Interesting, Be Interested."

- Dale Carnegie

Creating During Quarantine: What I Learned About Creating Together While We Were Apart

Social distancing, Zoom meetings, online shows . . . the disconnection we are facing in the world today can really have a powerful effect on creativity, so it's important to be willing to create differently. A few things make this possible: thinking a few steps ahead, expanding through limitations, and letting what's happening in the world play a part in what you're creating.

Here's an example of questions you can ask yourself to help you work creatively while you're apart:

Think A Few Steps Ahead

Ask Yourself: Where could this go wrong and what can I provide or how can I prevent that from happening?

When you're working with others, it doesn't hurt to consider what might be missing or preventing them from succeeding. And this means guessing where the potential pitfalls and holes in communication might be lurking.

"I've been reckless, but I'm not a rebel without a cause."

– Angelina Jolie

Working apart means there is less time or opportunity for the back and forth that happens during in-person collaboration, so you have to be ready to streamline processes. You need to be clear about action steps, communicate effectively, and think a few steps ahead about areas where there could be hiccups.

When I was directing Dancing Together Apart and editing together twenty different videos from twenty different dancers, there was room for a lot of variation: different cameras, different aesthetics, different ways of working. I knew that, on the one hand, the variety of styles and voices was what would make this piece strong and interesting, and yet at the same time, it could also be its downfall if not done well. Without some guidelines and organization, the result could feel non-cohesive, jumbled, or simply unprofessional.

How I handled it:

I knew I had to be very organized. As soon as I had the process for how we were going to pass the project along, I documented it and then communicated it in several different ways (Facebook group, meetings, person to person) at several different points. There were clear tech specs on camera angle, type of camera, length of shot, etc.

Also, about halfway through the project, I noticed that not everyone was able to perfectly replicate the ending pose of the person before them. As a result, I started sending screenshots of the final pose and articulating it in a way they could replicate without overthinking it (i.e., "You will need to begin with your right arm up and your left arm down, your body is flat to the camera, your chin is turned over your right shoulder . . . ," etc.) This gave each dancer the best shot at getting it right, and it also made it easy to give the film a seamless feeling in editing.

> *You want to set people up for success. Give your collaborators the information that they need to know so they can fulfill their role like a rock star and still have room to feel creative and in control of their part.*

Expand Through Limitations

Ask Yourself: How can I not only work in this new way or with these new restrictions, but actually make the most of this new way/format?

When forced to adapt quickly to working apart, it can feel like the rug has been pulled out from under us. The tendency is to focus on the pain of working in this new environment or bemoan the way things used to be. But there can be many rich opportunities for innovation when you choose to focus on what you're gaining in a new medium or mode of working as opposed to what you're losing.

> **Anyone can dwell on what's no longer available or possible, but to be a game-changer, you must forget about what was and focus on what is becoming.**

When the shelter-in-place orders first started happening and comedians were forced out of comedy clubs and public venues, they started setting up online Zoom comedy shows instead. Almost immediately, groans and complaints could be heard throughout the comedy community about this new medium: the audience's laughter either wasn't heard (they were muted) or it was too loud and distracting. The comics complained that this wasn't "real" stand up. Many of them simply stopped performing.

How I Handled It:

While I admit that Zoom comedy isn't the same as in-person stand-up shows, I immediately started looking for ways to make it work: asking audience members to comment in the chat, spotlighting the comic's video but unmuting the audience, and asking comics to make sure they have a good connection, a decent microphone, and an uncluttered background. What I found is that there are things that you can do in Zoom comedy that you can't do in regular stand-up! You can share your screen and include short videos or PowerPoint presentations as part of your act, you can greet every audience member by name, you can use wild virtual backgrounds. And I noticed facial expressions were now more visible onscreen than on stage, so I began to make use of that by allowing myself to be more subtle or taking moments to look directly into the camera lens.

I decided to treat a Zoom comedy show like interactive TV, and I started taking inspiration from comedy shows like SNL, Late Night, and other formats to inform what would and wouldn't work.

Let What's Happening In the World Play a Part in What You're Creating

Ask Yourself: How is my work affected by world events? How does it take part, challenge, concur, or reflect on what's going on around me?

No one makes art in a bubble. You are affected and connected to the world around you, and that's going to show up in whatever you're creating (no matter how loosely or how subconsciously). You don't have to be political, and you don't have to wrap your work up with current events, but you should at least be aware of how your work is responding to it all.

It's worth considering what part you're playing in what's going on around you and then communicate that to your audience. Some things are better left unsaid, but it can help your work be more well-received and more shared if people know how to contextualize it or are clear about its importance.

"There is a reason for the rebels to make a move and for the government to try to prevent that."
– Suliman Baldo

How We Handled It:

Making Dancing Together Apart began as a response to the pandemic, but it evolved into a reflection of the times and the movements the world is experiencing on a larger scale: namely the murder of George Floyd and the protests of the Black Lives Matter movement.

As the dancers started this project, the question was: "How can we work together while we are apart?" But as they witnessed the murder of George Floyd and the resulting protests, a more sobering question came to the surface: "How can we heal from the spaces that already exist between us?" With this in mind, we found ourselves offering this piece of art not only as a reflection of the times, but also with the hope that it opened hearts, sparked conversations, and provided a catalyst for change at the unconscious level in our viewers.

As the protests of the Black Lives Matter movement began to surge, many of the dancers got directly involved in supporting the movement in various ways—marching, protesting, running fundraising events—and some of the later pieces in

"Rebels and non-conformists are often the pioneers and designers of change."
– Indira Gandhi

the film reflect that. The final "mask reveal" shot lingers on the tearful face of dancer and contributing editor, Kimeiko Rae Vision, ending the piece in a poignant and moving finish that dares you to look away. While we didn't intend for the piece to be "about" the Black Lives Matter movement, we didn't resist when it began to weave itself in there. We allowed current events and the world we were living in to be a part of the work, if not at the center of it.

When creating in the middle of madness, it's OK to ask the questions:

What does this piece have to do with what's going on in the world right now? How am I being influenced, even vaguely?

Where do world events affect the creative process? How is that reflected in the final product?

The beautiful thing is that as you reflect on these things, there are no perfect or complete answers. The work itself doesn't have to be an answer, but it can be a journey down the path of the question. In other words . . .

You don't have to know the answers, you just need to ask the questions.

Your Love & Fear Elixir: What things aren't you able to do anymore? What are some things that you can do now that you couldn't before? What are some new or inventive things you've seen other people doing in an effort to create in challenging circumstances? What could you take away from that and try on your own? If you're collaborating with others, how can you support people by giving them all the information they might need to create without you successfully? How are world events showing up—even subtly— in the work you are creating now? How is that informing the flow, the subject, your thoughts?

The Rebel can be a powerful ally to your projects involving social justice. It's OK to use their anger and feistiness as a catalyst for your creativity.

Creating to Overcome Fear: You Already Know How to Do This

When the world is throwing you madness curveballs, when your entire revenue stream fizzles, when your job disappears, when the very pillars you depend on—like freedom, democracy, justice—seem to be compromised everywhere you look, it's easy to shrink and become inflexible. There is so much evidence that things are going wrong! Best to cling to what we have! In these cases, our minds want to dart away from the present moment (where we are most creative) to the future (where we are not). We play out worst-case scenarios of what might happen, or we retreat into the past and search for answers as to how we got here. We might even feel ourselves give in to feelings of despair . . . Everything is ruined now, why even try!

But as artists, this isn't something we haven't faced before. In fact, probably many times before . . .

Have you ever had something go wrong in the middle of a performance? Something doesn't go as planned. A prop isn't where it needs to be, or another musician forgets the changes you made during rehearsal, or your scene partner skips ahead and says a different line. It may not be disastrous on a worldwide level, but it can feel that way in the moment. But if you've managed to work through these situations, it's likely because you were able to use the attributes of Creativity—saying yes, listening to the good voice in your head, and playing the game in front of you.

What's Happening When Something Goes Wrong

When something "goes wrong," it only means that something went differently than expected and we're afraid that we're not going to have the resources to pull through. It's challenging you to access your creativity and ever flowing abundance of ideas. It can only be through accepting the imperfection and creating around it, with it, and through it that we've been able to make our way through these seemingly disastrous situations.

Many, many years ago, I was directing a company and watching the players get ready before curtain. This one dancer was practicing her steps again and again and again, and I could see this worry mounting on her face as she was practicing this one part. Being a director, I wanted to put her in a good mood right before she went onstage as opposed to stressing over every little detail. At this point in the game, it was too late to try to perfect something that wasn't already fixed, so I put my hands on her shoulders and I told her what I'd been told by another director years before:

"Something will go wrong and you're going to be just fine."

That's what I want to tell you as well. Because chances are, if you've performed or lived life at all, something has gone wrong. Something has viciously marred the perfection of your work, and you've survived it. Not only survived it, but perhaps you've even made gold out of it.

Consider how you practice: I often tell actors that practice is not about becoming perfect, but rather knowing how to deal with imperfection when it comes up. And I would go so far as to say that it's even more than just dealing with the imperfection—it's about turning it into creative genius. Genius is when a mistake happens, and instead of freaking out, you find a way to work it in. Now that is pure genius!

Consider your collaborators and the people who hire you: Casting directors and producers want to work with artists who aren't going to freak out when something doesn't go right. They want professionals who are going to recompose themselves, make the best of it, and move on. Extreme perfectionists are exhausting to work with. Chances are, if people like working with you, you've figured out how to go with the flow. The creative flow.

A Note About Perfection - it's not as attractive as you think

When I coach Hollywood actors, I often find that there's this prevailing hope that if they could just overcome their nerves and their flop sweating that they could nail it and do it "right." But this is setting them up for failure.

There is no such thing as repeating a "perfect" performance. You're holding on too tightly to something that's already passed for fear you won't come up with anything better; but trying to re-create exactly what you did yesterday is without a doubt going to leave you coming up short of yesterday's brilliance. Each performance must be found anew, and mistakes have to be not only accepted but used as an incredible, wonderful, surprising gift! It's about being resourceful and using what's right in front of you.

Here's what's up: When you make a mistake, in that moment that you fumble, you are your most alive. I know perfectionists out there that are reading this don't want to hear this, so let me just repeat it.

When you make a mistake you are your most alive . . . and therefore, the most captivating.

So many of our most brilliant moments, our most honest moments, our most tender moments—these are the moments when something unexpected happens. These are the moment where the audience gets to see a flash of something they recognize—and sometimes that could be what is otherwise known as a mistake. So in your artistic life, just as in your work itself . . .

You aren't preparing to be perfect.

You are preparing how to make genius out of non-perfection.

Say you are auditioning for a film and you drop a line. You pause. There is a beat of silence where you're figuring out how to handle it. It's in this moment that the room crackles with "aliveness" because the future of that moment is unknown. The casting director looks up, leans in, waiting.

Now there are two outcomes to this scenario. In one, you are extremely apologetic:

Oh, whoops! So, so sorry. Is it OK if I take it back? Ummmm, just let me get back here. . . Where was I? Oh, I'm confused. I'm sorry, there was traffic on the way over and I just feel so ruffled, um. .

Or there's another scenario where you handle it like a pro:

Ok, right. Taking it back. . . [Repeats last line and continues seamlessly]

And finally there's another scenario where you figure out a way to make yourself right and you handle it like a master:

Silence. Making the beat right for the scene. Staying in character. Improvising. Or finding the next line from that new silence. Discovering something new in the character simply because you were forced by this wonderful, surprise gift of a "mistake."

When a mistake happens, you must learn to embrace it and say to yourself, Ok, cool, what now?

Guess who the casting directors want to hire in this case? Do they want to hire the person who is caught up in their own emotions, making excuses, spinning a story about it and wasting everyone's time? Or do they want the person who makes great creative work that no one could have planned for simply because they forgot a line? Yep, they want the creative master who works with the tools they have in the moment.

The Rebel likes a little chaos, but they want to be the creators of it. So you might find your Rebel acting up when things go unplanned. They'll want you to throw up your hands, quit, throw a fit. In these moments, you must coax your Rebel to go along for the ride and convince them that this could actually be fun.

> Amateurs make mistakes.
> Masters seize the mistakes and mold it into genius.

All this to say that the end goal in learning to work with your fear and use it onstage is not to become perfect. It's actually quite the opposite. It's to embrace your humanity. That thing that makes you imperfect also makes you riveting to watch. Your fear inserts itself into the room with you, elbows its way to the forefront, and demands to be seen. Work with it as a partner and you'll be amazed what this energy of fear can do for you. Push against it and see how it rules you.

The gift of something going "wrong" can throw us into the present moment—but only if we allow it. We must deal, we must cope. It's a fire we have to put it out. And by saying 'yes' to the experience, keeping our creative voice channels open and playing the game in front of us—just as we do on stage and in our artistic lives—we are often gifted with a flood of never-before tapped creativity.

Exercising Your Creativity in the Face of the Heckler

The Rebel often manifests not just through us as our shadow self but through our audiences as the heckler, the person who walks out in the middle of your performance, who yawns during your big speech, and who only has negative things to say on your posts. While often disruptive and rattling, they're also a great teacher when it comes to being creative in the moment. The exercise below uses the heckler as a provocateur to help you learn how to stay in the moment and continue to say 'yes' without giving up your power as leader of the room.

In a group or pairs, take turns performing a three-five minute piece of memorized or prepared material:

The person who is performing runs through their set, and as they do they are heckled by the members of the audience (i.e., the other members of the group). The person performing somehow has to find a way to deal with it, stay in the moment, and move on. There are a million different ways to deal with a heckler without totally derailing. Remember that you as the performer, as the person with the microphone and lights, you're the most powerful person in the room. That is your role. So, without giving up your power to the heckler, explore ways you can say yes to it, incorporate it, or keep flowing.

"The new rebels might be artists willing to risk the yawn, the rolled eyes, the cool smile, the nudged ribs, the parody of gifted ironists, the oh how banal."

\- David Foster Wallace

Things the Pretend Audience Hecklers Can Do:

- Laugh too loudly
- Laugh in the wrong place (when something isn't funny, or during seri ous parts)
- Have a coughing fit
- Pretend your performer is really boring, sigh loudly, look away, make disruptive noises
- Get up and look for your keys or missing object on the floor
- Say things, "Oh hell no!" and shake your head in disagreement
- Start clapping at an inappropriate moment

- Nod furiously in agreement and make loud noises of approval for lengths of time. (While on the one hand you're saying 'yes' to the performance in a supportive way, you are also disrupting the flow by making yourself too much a part of the show.)

- Pretend to have headphones on and dance in your seat

- Say "What?" at different times like you can't understand what's going on

- Get into a loud, heated, whispering conversation with the audience member sitting next to you

- Throw something to another member of the audience a few rows away

Note About Doing this Exercise Virtually: When I did this exercise in my online incubator workshop, I had participants go into breakout rooms of three-four people. From my position as the person running the Zoom meeting, I was able to broadcast messages to the members of the group. I would feed the pretend audience members these ideas above one by one in order to prompt them to do the heckling.

The Rebel can show up not only in you, but also outside of you. The heckler in the audience, the person who yawns, or tries to divert attention to themselves, this is The Rebel reflected on the outside where you can dance opposite them. In making peace with them there, it changes something inside of you as well.

Is It Really Ok to Say "Yes"?

When I get to the topic of creativity and saying "yes," there is sometimes an argument that sounds like this:

> But does saying "yes" and turning in the direction of ease instead of resistance mean I'm burying my head in the sand?

From the outside, saying "yes" can appear to be a Pollyanna or a privileged perspective. And so, I want to be clear that I'm not advocating for turning a blind eye to those in need or to the problems of the world. I'm advocating for choosing a better lens when you approach these things.

Let's go back to the airplane situation. When we are in panic, we don't function well. Imagine if I had given into the fear and started yelling or crying? What if I had followed the conflict by starting to think of all the ways in which we could fall out of the sky, imagining all the people in my life who would be affected by my death? I would have been no use to anyone, and it wouldn't have helped at all.

Saying "yes" to everything is a way of seeing (not denying) what is happening and then asking, "OK, so this is happening, so now what?"

It's following up on the truth with positive action.

It's steering into the waves because it's the most helpful thing to do.

Once we accept where we are, then we can come up with solutions when they are needed.

"Rebels are the people who refuse the seen for the unseen."

\- Anne Douglas Sedgwick

Part III

Dealing with the Fear of The Unknown

Fear of The Unknown

Also Known As: Fear of powerlessness, death, old age

Mindset: Control

Shadow Self: The Fabulist

Adrenaline Response: Freeze

Mode of Operation: Contraction

Key for Evolution: Letting go or expansion

Limiting Belief: "I'm not sure what's around the corner, so maybe if I do nothing, I'll stay safe."

Manifests As: Worry, perfectionism, inaction, indecisiveness, over-preparation, obsessive behavior, living in the future instead of the present

New Belief: "I trust that I'm equipped to deal with whatever is coming next and that everything is always working out in my favor."

Trust In: Good universe

Connect: With your present surroundings

Create: Deliberately create in the moment. Experiences of imperfection, messiness, and carefreeness that have only mild or little consequences.

New Story: "There is nothing to be gained by worrying about the future when my power is in the powerful present. Things are always working out for me."

Repeat Daily: "The future is just a present moment I haven't created yet."

Angel wakes up every morning and does the same exact routine: gets up and puts on the kettle, meditates for five minutes until it comes to a boil, counts out one cup exactly of oatmeal to microwave, showers while it heats, then eats while reviewing the score they're working on. Once done eating they practice for 90 minutes, then they spend about 10 minutes getting out the door (keys, violin, wallet, bus pass? check!) and begin their day out in the world. The routine, though full of great habits that support them in a healthy lifestyle, also borders a little on the obsessive compulsive. A quality that has served them well in the classical music world has an extra baggage of anxiety that goes with it. When we begin to work together, Angel has hit a slump in success: they've made it into a world class orchestra as a regular sub but don't seem to be able to move up into one as a permanent position. After years of trying for seats and not getting one they come to see me. They've been told their rigidity bleeds into their music and that they could benefit from "loosening up a bit." While highly perfunctory and technical, their playing has also been called by harsher colleagues as "unfeeling."

Angel is particularly hard on themselves when they make a mistake - which is often because absolute perfection is always the goal. Note for note, tone for tone, they are required and trained to play the music exactly as it is written and yet they've become so inflexible in this attitude that they also have a hard time recovering quickly when they make a mistake. A half second blip causes their nervous system to go into a panic, they go flush and begin to sweat and while they're able to continue playing they find themselves detached from the playing and still worrying about their mistake.

This pattern has begun to cause dread about performances. Anytime the orchestra has a performance coming up, they begin to worry for days in advance never knowing when they will need to step in, never knowing when they'll be called to sub - and so they practice until it's perfect and then they practice more.

Indicators of Fear of The Unknown

Worry

If you are plagued by this fear, then you might find yourself being a worrier. Having a disproportionate amount of concern about the future means that if you don't know what's happening next, then your mind instinctively grapples with different scenarios. You imagine all the worst outcomes more than the best. Your imagination accepts the momentum of these suggestions of "what if," and eventually the scenes become so vivid and detailed that they begin to feel like the real thing.

Perfectionism

In order to manage your worry, you search for places where you have control. You think that if you can hold yourself to a higher and higher standard, then you will at least have some effect on the outcome, and so perfectionism follows. What begins as a not-altogether-unhealthy impulse can quickly spiral out of control.

Over-Preparation and Obsessive Behavior

Perfectionism leads to over-preparation and obsessive behavior. You practice until it isn't fun anymore. From that negative mood, it's easy to slide into self-doubt. You practice until you begin to doubt that your practicing is helping anything. You start to wonder if you can control anything at all, and so you come up with obsessive actions based on very arbitrary rules. These obsessive actions have an almost magical-reality quality. They may or may not lead to success, but you feel some sense of calm from having fulfilled the task.

Self-Punishment

Obsessive tasks can also be used to inflict self-punishment when you don't reach the high standards you set for yourself. Your set didn't close with laughter and applause? Your punishment is to go home and write 100 closer jokes. A certain section of the musical interlude didn't pop with the same chemistry as before? You spend all night revising it and re-doing it, convinced that you can still do better, sometimes driving your co-drivers or collaborators crazy.

Inaction and Indecisiveness

Instead of perfectionism and over-preparation, sometimes the fear of the unknown can lead to a freeze response where you find yourself unsure what action to take and unable to make a move. You are so worried about the worst outcome that you do nothing at all. You become a prisoner of your worst what-if scenarios. At the very least, you feel like if you just stay put, then you won't have to take responsibility for what comes next.

Feeling Like You Are The Unknown

The more you fail to live up to your high perfectionist standards—or conversely, the more you are frozen into inaction—the more you begin to doubt yourself and your ability to control anything, even yourself. Instead of embracing and finding the beauty in your humanity, you loathe your own incalculability. You deny your shadow side and therefore grow farther and farther apart from your full self. You become unknown to yourself.

Living in the Future

Just as the fear of not enough can get you stuck in the past, the fear of the "unknown" sticks you solidly in the future. Your mind becomes so obsessed with the gaping hole that is the unknown that it constantly tries to fill it in. You may find yourself constantly playing out different scenarios or losing trust of those around you because "you can already see how this is going to play out." Without meaning to, you miss what's happening in the present moment because you're so concerned with what's next. People may rely on you (you're great at planning), but they don't always enjoy you. They get the sense you're living in your mind, far away, somewhere else.

When confronted with painful situations you can't control, there is one shadow self who will attempt to "save" you from the unsettling truth. It will try to protect you with its ability to distort and deny—but when called out for its deception, it will continue to dig in its heels and sow layers of confusion.

> **This third shadow self twists and turns from the harsh glare of truth because it's guarding your reputation. Meet the Fabulist.**

Signs That You Are Allowing
The Fear of The Unknown to Run You

You are sick often, you over-prepare for everything, you have a hard time listening or being in the present moment, you are obsessive-compulsive, you take a long time to make decisions. You often feel as though you've failed or not measured up to expectations. Fear of the unknown manifests in one of two ways: Either you are someone who is so set on the future (and how you want it to turn out) that you are always trying to control the outcome and often feeling disappointed, or you are someone who feels so out of control in their life that they're always fearing what's around the corner and distrusting the outcome. Fear of the unknown elicits either an attempt to over-control things or a relinquishing, a sort of giving up of one's power.

Your Shadow Self: The Fabulist

The shadow self that arises out of the fear of the unknown is the Fabulist.

When I told the woman sitting next to me on the airplane, "Oh, I've been on lots of bumpy flights," that was the Fabulist telling a little harmless lie to soothe someone else. That's the Fabulist at their best. At their worst, the Fabulist would simply have denied that there was any crisis at all. The pilot tells everyone to buckle up and they yell out "Fake news!" And then demand to get up and use the bathroom.

At their best, the Fabulist is someone who makes up stories because they feel good, because it is more fun to do so—or at least less painful. We are natural born Fabulists. Around the age of three, children begin to lie for a variety of reasons, one of which is that they are experimenting with trying on stories they've heard. Another reason is because they are pretending they've experienced something which they haven't. These relatively harmless "tall tales" are common, but all too often rejected. We are quick to rush in and say to them, "Tell the truth! Be honest!"

"Oh, what a tangled web we weave, when first we practice to deceive!"

- Sir Walter Scott

Honesty is an important value, because without it, the very fabric of societal trust is demolished. In the beginning of our lives, we experiment, we deceive our parents, we duck out of responsibility, but ultimately most of us settle into a life of little white lies to protect people's feelings, or the occasional exaggeration of this detail or that in our storytelling. The Fabulist may make life seem rosier or heighten the drama at times, but for most of us it stays relatively tame.

As young artists, we often exercised our tall-tale-telling by stretching our imaginations into far reaching places, constantly asking "why not?" and "what if?". Seeing things differently than they really are is a great skill for an artist, but it gets dangerous when it leaks into regular life. When this happens, the line between reality and imagination can get blurred in such a way to make people distrust you. When things get difficult, or when we fail, we may access the Fabulist to make ourselves feel better.

"A liar deceives himself more than anyone, for he believes he can remain a person of good character when he cannot."

- Richelle E. Goodrich

At their worst, this shadow self manifests as an outright liar, fabricating whole truths, changing the terms on you, and gaslighting in an unabashed effort to get their way. They don't care how the stories they make up affect others, they just delight in the telling of them.

The Fabulist gives themselves license to stretch the truth, to bend perception, and sometimes even to manipulate the truth in their favor. They deny the hard objectivity of truth. What can be entertaining in the right contexts (like in art), or helpful in others (therapeutic re-tellings of trauma, for instance), can also be dangerously disruptive when used to distort reality and manipulate people. Lies are one of the best ways to cause confusion and thusly fear. When we feel a break in the fabric of what we can trust, then we can longer trust anything at all.

The Fabulist is attractive because of the web of charm they can spin. They don't want to give up the ability to use filters and camera angles to make themselves appear the most attractive. Deeply imbedded in vanity, the Fabulist is one of the most dangerous of shadow selves. Creating a "web" that is hard to unweave, they shake the foundation of everyone's else's understanding of truth in an effort to divert the blame away from themselves. The more they lie, the harder it is to escape. They know the moment they accept the invitation to align with the truth, they'll be seen as they really are—and subconsciously they despise themselves most of all.

Appeasing The Fabulist:	Fabulists have to find their own trustworthy crew that holds them accountable—but in a loving way, and without judgement. Their ability to weave stories and look at things with a new perspective can be excellent for morale or extremely valuable for creative solution-oriented thinking. When accessed, the Fabulist makes an excellent leader because people are bewitched by their charm and story-telling skills.
Important to The Fabulist:	Image, entitlement, illusion of safety
How The Fabulist Handles Fear:	Denial. "Fear? What fear? Everything's just fine!"
Admired for:	Their charm, their seeming ability to have it all figured out.
The Fabulist says:	"It basically means the same thing," "It's some of the truth," or whatever makes them feel better.
Famous Fabulist:	Scheherazade, Richard Nixon, Rachel Dolezal,Chicken Little, The Boy Who Cried Wolf

Your Love & Fear Elixir: How does the Fabulist play out in your life? Where do you bend the truth for convenience, vanity, or to save yourself some emotional effort? Was there ever a time you were caught in a lie? How did you respond? Where do you allow yourself to tell white lies? When do you lie to yourself? About what? Is there anything that you lie about to yourself the most?

Crafting Story: Deciding Where You'll Go

In these times when we are faced with the fear of the unknown, when it feels like the world is thrust into madness, what can be most disturbing is the loss of control. It can feel like we're living in our worst imagined nightmare and the sensation of losing our grip on the wheel can give us emotional whiplash. We feel tossed around at the mercy of world events, at the mercy of others, at the mercy of the unknown. And in an effort to soothe ourselves, we will sometimes grasp onto the first story we come across. We want to explain things. We want to be locked into a narrative, no matter how destructive or unhelpful, so we can regain a sense of knowing where we are headed.

Story is the gift our imaginations has given us for overcoming fear . . . or provoking it.

It's one of your most combustible tools to deal with fear because it either improves it or adds to it. It's like a fire that can ignite a piece of dynamite or turn a piece of bread into toast. It has the power to explode or transform – it can do either one depending on you.

Our brains are hard-wired for story. This means that we glom onto stories and listen more deeply when we hear them. When we come upon something that we don't understand or that is challenging, our brains begin to try to make sense of it— and so we make up a story about it. This can work in our favor (when we make up a positive reason or story for something) or it can work against us (when we assume the worst or make up a negative reason for something).

"You, like every human being, are a storyteller by birthright. Ask that all who gather at your fire come with goodwill to share their truths in its warmth."

- Nancy Mellon

When fear is unchecked, these negative stories can become very damaging and may seem very real to us. For example, if we have a history of getting nervous before a big performance, we may feel shaky in the knees or a little nauseous. We may not be able to control these responses, but if we tell ourselves things like "Oh no! It's happening again, I'll never be able to control this! What if I mess up?" then we begin adding momentum to the fear. We make it bigger, and we make our symptoms bigger, too.

Of all the damaging things we do with fear, the most damaging is when we use it as evidence to back up false stories. Stories like:

"Oh, maybe this means that I'm not good enough."

"Maybe I have this fear because I'm not really meant to do this."

"I always do this and I always fail, and now I'm going to mess up and embarrass myself . . . this is the worst day ever!"

Consider this story I keep telling you about stage fright:

When you have any of the symptoms of stage fright—shaking, rapid heartbeat, nausea, sweating—it doesn't mean you shouldn't be doing this. It means that you should. It means there is an energy that is trying to come through you and to you, but it's up to you to get up to speed with it. It's up to you to tell a different story about it.

Often, my clients' biggest and most helpful revelation is reframing the fight-flight-or-freeze response into something useful, and even beneficial and pleasurable. They find that when they change their story about what is happening, then it changes the way they feel about it.

You get to decide what story you're telling about your symptoms of fear—of any kind. You have the power to reframe them in a way that serves you. You can tell new stories about how you got here, why you're here, and how the rest of it is going to go.

Taking Fear By the Reins

When we use storytelling to reframe our situation, we are taking fear by the reins. We are allowing the energy in but redirecting its route. The fear is like a wild horse: while we have control of it, it can power a large wagon to move very fast, but if we don't have control of it, we're at the mercy of where it wants to go, and the ride can be chaotic and dangerous.

When we craft, we choose. When we choose, we take control over what's happening to us.

Positioning Your Past

Ali is a powerhouse on the piano. Anytime they sit down to play, a rush of improvisation pours forth in a torrent of emotion with melodies rising and falling, changing, morphing - and this constant creative flow stretches out for an hour or two at a time. And yet they're really hesitant to commit themselves to making work regularly. They're down for any jam session but they didn't see how they would ever be able to produce an album. In their mind it was inevitable that they would always just be a jam player, relinquishing the chance their work would ever be captured in fuller form. "I just don't think I have it in me to commit and produce a whole album," they say.

After working with them for some time, it's clear that somewhere along the way they'd been told they were flaky and not talented enough times that they started to believe it. It started with their dad who would complain when they would just "fool around" on the piano instead of doing the regimented piano practice exercises. Growing bored with the repetition of scales, their fingers would eventually wander and get creative, eliciting shouts of disapproval from the other room. Then in high school they became distracted by romance and the usual teen stuff. A couple of missed deadlines for showcases made the music teacher scowl at them. And even though they were always able to boot-strap it through a performance on their talent and improvisational skills alone, they were admonished, skipped over for opportunities and berated for not being "committed enough." So much so that by the time they were an adult and actually ready to start taking responsibility they already had a story of themselves in their head of being a flake. Through working together over several months, we unwound some of these beliefs, and looked for evidence of a different story. It turned out, Ali is actually quite consistent in showing up to their 9-5 job, remembering friends' birthdays. Building on that and healing the past, Ali has been able to choose a new lens to see themselves through and finally began producing albums.

We can't change the past, but we can change our re-telling of it. Doing this for therapeutic reasons is called the Narrative Therapy Technique in Positive Psychology. It uses re-authoring to re-tell something that has already happened in order to tell a new story about what will happen. So, where you might feel powerless in a situation that happened in the past, you can use this technique to help you shape your thoughts around it and find an empowering stance to move forward. It doesn't try to mask the facts of what actually happened (as in denial), but rather changes how you feel about what happened. You create your own meaning and purpose about the past rather than searching for an absolute truth that doesn't work for you.

The great thing about this re-telling of the past is that can take the negative charge out of those experiences. As you begin crafting your own stories, start by answering a few questions to pinpoint of few notable or meaningful experiences for yourself.

"You have to begin to tell the story of your life as you now want it to be and discontinue the tales of how it has been or of how it is."

– Esther and Jerry Hicks

Questions to Begin Re-Shaping Your Past

Fear of the Unknown: What is the story you're telling about what might happen? Is this honestly the only outcome? If the outcome could be different, what would you like it to be? Once you know that outcome, ask yourself: are there any possible ways forward that could start me on the path towards that? What might those changes be?

Fear of The Other: What is the story you're telling about other people? Is it a fair assessment? Where might you be making assumptions or exaggerating something in your mind that might be not true?

Fear of Not Enough: What is the story you're telling about your worth? How do you feel about yourself, and where do you think it started? See if you can identify where that critical voice is coming from. A teacher, parent, lover, sibling, person in your life? What if they got it horribly wrong? What if they had said something different in that moment? What might that have been that you would have liked to hear instead?

Tell A New Story . . . And Make It Good

Crafting a new story is often the hardest thing for people to do. You have probably gone a very long time with certain decisions about yourself or the world and making an abrupt pivot can be difficult to do—and difficult to stick to. It can be tricky to imagine something that you don't already feel about yourself or another person or a situation.

I find it helpful to use those devices, guidelines, and prompts we might normally use to write a story in order to re-shape our own. Where our brains want to revolt against changing the narrative, we must inject fun, playfulness, and creativity! In the following sections, I'll share different approaches for crafting your story that will gameify the process and direct your boundless imagination for the better.

The Fabulist wants to retell your past to make you look good. I want you to retell your past to make you feel better. To forgive yourself, to surrender your heartache, or the anger standing in your way. You must engage the Fabulist to use their talent not to lie about the past, but to give it a new, loving perspective so you can move forward from it.

Seeing Your Life Like a Story-boarding Artist

In the world of filmmaking, the storyboard artist is the one who maps out the plan visually after the script is written. They have to be aware of the different "shots" or camera angles they can use as they draw the different scenes. Using the language of the storyboard artist, let's explore the different perspectives you can take when looking at your story and re-shaping your past:

Establishing Shot

The establishing shot is the shot you often see at the beginning or ending of a segment that orients the audience. For example, the shot of the outside of the house at the start of a sitcom: it lets us know a little bit more about the place, culture, and world we are peeking into. So, if you were watching the movie of your life now or the situations you want to reframe, what would the establishing shot be? Where are you in space, place, and time? Where are you located? What is your scenery like? The world around you? Just as the establishing shot in films helps the audience understand where the story is taking place, this view also helps you understand the context of the story you've been living and your relationship to the other things in your immediate world.

Wide Shot

Now we move into the characters and what's going on with them. The wide shot includes the key characters and the space where they're living. It gives room for action. So, if you were watching the movie of your life, how does it look? What do you see that you might not have noticed before? What's different when you can see all the action going on at once as though from the perspective of a viewer?

Medium Shot

The medium shot moves in on the characters. There's still room for action, but we see more of the expression and the emotion. So, as you're imagining this movie of your life, ask yourself: What are the emotional arcs happening between you and others? What is the emotional undercurrent that's happening, the back and forth beyond the actions?

Close-Up

The close-up shot in film is when the camera moves in closer to one character and we often find out new information about how they really feel (or maybe inside information that the other character doesn't know). In the scene of your life, see if you can move that proverbial "camera" in closer on yourself. How do you really feel about what's happening?

Extreme Close-Up

The extreme close-up shot is just like it sounds: the camera moves in super close. In film, this is done to draw attention to something we may have missed before. Sometimes it's a discovery about something the character is feeling that even they aren't aware of. So, as the "camera" draws even closer, ask yourself: Is there something I'm missing? Where am I fooling myself or telling a story that isn't quite the truth? Where am I opting for a comfortable version of something? Where am I missing something? Could I be wrong about what is happening?

Over the Shoulder

You'll often see this shot used in film and television when two characters are in a conversation. We see the conversation from over the shoulder of one character, and then we switch and see it from over the shoulder of the other. As you are viewing your life, how can you see conflicts and exchanges from both sides? Can you switch your perspective to that of the other person and see what that experience is like? What's it like to be in a conversation with you? On the other side of you in an emotional argument? A deep discussion? A moment of intense longing? How can you see it through the other person's eyes?

Back View

The back view is when the camera is only capturing the backside of a character and we are directed towards whatever they are looking at. In that moment, we are imagining what they must be feeling because we can't see it on their face. If you saw yourself through someone else's eyes, where do they see you looking? What do you have in front of you? What's got your attention? What are you facing? And how do you feel about your view? What's your emotional connection or reaction to what's right in front of you?

Crowd's View

When the camera captures a crowd of people, rarely is it without having some central focus. They eye is naturally searching for a resting point, and subconsciously we ask, "Who is the leader of this mob?" See yourself as you are positioned among many others. Where are you part of the crowd and where are you a leader? Now put yourself as the focal point in a crowd. Is the crowd for you or against you? What's your role in community? How can you see yourself as a leader among many, and what are you doing at the helm?

Up Shot

The up shot is where the camera is below the character and we see them sort of looming in the frame. It's used to emphasize their largeness, their power, or their heroic qualities. What if you were to look at yourself as though you were a hero in this situation? What does it look like to see yourself as champion of the challenges in your life? How can you reframe some of your actions to see them as aiding the situation—or doing your best to save yourself (or others)—rather than in a negative light?

Down Shot

Conversely, the down shot is where the camera is slightly above the character and looking down at them. When we think of "looking down" on someone, it is often used in a negative way to mean they are lesser than us, but this shot can also be used to emphasize fragility or vulnerability. So, what if you were to view your situation or the movie of your life as though you were a child? Where do you need to let yourself off the hook a bit by recognizing your challenges, vulnerabilities, and weaknesses? Where can you see that you are/were in the process of learning or growing just as a child does?

Bird's Eye View

The bird's eye view, or sometimes called "The God Shot," is when we are looking things from high above. It's a detached perspective where you rise up out of the visceral emotion of something. Imagine you're God looking down at yourself and see yourself from this higher, more loving perspective. What can you see now that you might have missed below? How does this event fit into a larger context of the world around you? Of humanity? Where can you start to see yourself and others with more forgiving eyes?

Once you're able to see a situation from all these different perspectives, it will naturally begin to shift some of that emotional charge inside of you. Emotions are like mud—they get stuck to us, but if we're willing to poke them, inspect them, and move them around, then they can't help but shake loose.

Your Mission, Should You Choose To Accept It: Take out a piece of paper and write out these different perspectives in a list, leaving space in between. Get a past memory in your mind that you'd like to work with. Now close your eyes and imagine it. How do you see it at first? From which perspective? How does it look from that perspective? What things do you notice? Write them down next to that shot. Now do this for all of the shots, turning the picture in your mind of the memory and seeing it from all these different angles. Do them in the order they are listed above, ending with the bird's eye view. Now go back to your original perspective: has anything changed in how you see it?

"The story that you're living is the story you keep telling yourself, over and over. Start telling a better feeling story."

- Abraham Hicks

Writing Your Script with Pixar Wisdom

From the beginning, Pixar set itself apart in the world of animation because of its use of compelling storytelling in their films. Borrowing from some of their most relevant storytelling advice*, use their wisdom to guide your own storytelling.[1]

Pixar says, "Pull apart the stories you like. What you like in them is a part of you; you've got to recognize it before you can use it."

What are the stories you've always loved? From the fairytales you might have heard as a child, to books and movies you've always been drawn to. You might be surprised to find you have a certain mythological archetype you've been playing out all along. It's helpful to identify it because then you can decide if it's working for you or if you want to ditch that old story and find a new one. Look for characters that win your heart, inspire you, and make you feel stronger. And then see if you can recognize yourself in that character. Ask yourself, "What do we have in common?"

Pixar says, "Come up with your ending before you figure out your middle. Seriously. Endings are hard, get yours working up front."

Inevitability is the death of creativity. Many of us talk about a negative outcome as though it is inevitable, but what this does is cut off any opennesss to different possibilities. Sometimes we don't even realize we have an outcome in mind—we are just blindly following the path laid out for us, not cognizant of how this particular fairy tale ends. When we are crafting our story, we must deliberately start at the end. Start there and work your way backwards.

Ask yourself, "What outcome do I want?"

And then ask, "What is the story I need to be telling in order to reach that ending?"

When you ask the question, What would need to happen to make it so?, it puts you in a position of creativity instead of inevitability. And it helps you resonate with the solutions as opposed to being stuck in the rut of a linear path.

---

[1] Referenced from "22 Tips on the Pixar Storytelling Formula" which were originally Tweeted by Pixar's Story Artist, Emma Coats

Pixar says, "When you're stuck, make a list of what wouldn't happen next. Lots of times the material to get you unstuck will show up."

The creative mind works in mysterious ways, and sometimes naming the obvious answers can simply get your mind working and open you up to the answers you really want. Next time you feel like you can't imagine what you would do, simply ask yourself the opposite, "What won't I do? What would never happen? What is the most absurd, far out idea I can think of to resolve this?"

Pixar says, "You gotta identify with your situation/characters, can't just write 'cool'. What would make YOU act that way?"

If you're trying to paint yourself as a hero in a situation, take one step back and ask yourself what would make a hero, a cool guy, a funny gal, a likable person act that way? In your emulation of a type of person that has it together, you want to consider what things in their life make them act that way. Perhaps it's the support network they've put together for themselves, the way they structure their lives, the things they do, and the thoughts they think. Often what we see as "cool" or "confident" is the result of being in integrity with yourself. It is doing right by yourself and speaking kindly of yourself in your own head and to others. Being true to yourself starts with doing things that make you like who you see in the mirror. When reaching for a stronger you, ask yourself, "What do I need to be thinking, doing, saying in order to be this person?"

Pixar says, "Why must you tell THIS story? What's the belief burning within you that your story feeds off of? That's the heart of it."

Underneath any story that we've been telling ourselves is a deep-rooted belief, sometimes hiding in the shadows. It's hard to start changing your story if your belief is singing a different tune. Once you know what new story you want to be telling, make sure you ask yourself, "What do I have to believe in order to be living that reality truthfully?"

Pixar says, "You admire a character for trying more than for their success."

Are you a little bit of a drama mama? Well, there's a good reason why you might be more likely to share stories about your failures or challenges: people listen more. No one wants to hear the story of someone who is perfect or who managed to become successful with hardly any effort. That's not a good story! Most of us don't connect to that all that much.

Case in point, you had a really good day, got tons of work completed, got an email that you'd been accepted to that show you applied for—a totally in-the-flow day. But then on the way to the restaurant to meet friends, your ex-lover texts you an alarming text message saying that they would like to get together and "talk". What do you think you're going to be focused on when you get to that restaurant? Yep, it's most likely you'll tell the story that's got the most emotion and drama so you'll talk about the text from your ex. You see your friends eyes wandering around the room when you go into detail about how much you love your life. (Note: If you have excellent friends, they'll want to hear about the creative day more, but unfortunately that's not always the case—see the section on Collaborators: Your Creative Soulmates) You have a deep desire to connect and entertain, so you'll drift into the ex-story to retain that connection.

"I have learned that under certain circumstances, a fib is not only permissible, but can even be an act of perfect grace."

– Alan Bradley

Acting As If

Lastly, you can begin to tell a new story by acting "as if" you already have the life, the things, the relationships, the perspective that you want. It's a kind of "fake it till you make it" attitude. Acting as if works on the Law of Reversibility, which states that says that "if you feel a certain way, you will act in a manner consistent with that feeling." And the reverse is equally true: "If you act in a manner consistent with that feeling, even if you don't feel it, the Law of Reversibility will create the feeling that is consistent with your actions." In this way, by acting as if you already do not fear something, the fear itself eventually disappears.

Some Examples of Acting "As if"

Nervous you might mess up that audition? Act "as if" it isn't a big deal and you know you are going to nail it. Prepare for a good length of time—maybe an hour, but don't overdo it—and then let it go. Have breakfast with a friend, take your kid to school, get dressed with joyfulness, forget about the audition, and lead a good life! Then when it's time for the audition, you will be relaxed, more able to sink into the character, and have more energy to bring to the room.

Are you afraid of losing your job? Act "as if" the people you work for want to keep you forever. Plan your next project to bring to the team. Get a new chair for your desk. Take your work seriously and do it with care as though you personally own the company. They will feel your confidence and, if they were on the fence about you, your new attitude can shift the way they feel about you. They will feel your trust and it will help them to relax into their own.

Do you secretly fear that you won't be able to finish your next piece on time or be able to extract from it the pure genius that you hope for? Pretend that you can. Approach your day as though you're going to end satisfied. Bring all the things you would need to get lots of work done that day. Dress in clothes you feel great in. Bring your lunch so you don't have to leave. Clear all distractions and make sure people know not to disturb you—make way, people! Genius coming through!

> "Lady, I do not make up things. That is lies. Lies are not true. But the truth could be made if you know how. And that's the truth."
>
> - Lily Tomlin

Your Mission, Should You Choose to Accept It: In what area of your life might acting "as if" help you? What can you pretend in order to change your attitude or how you feel about it around? Try on this "new act" for a week and see how it goes.

"If you read folklore and mythology, any kind of myths, any kind of tall tales, running is always associated with freedom and vitality and youthfulness and eternal vigor. It's only in our lifetime that running has become associated with fear and pain."

\- Christopher McDougall

Crafting Story to Overcome Fear: You See? You Already Know How to Do This

If you've ever had a bad or mediocre performance (and I mean, really, who hasn't?), and you found a way to get back on stage and do it all again, it's because you were able to craft your story to overcome that fear of bombing again. You were able to find a way to feel secure that you could get a better grip on the wheel next time. You tightened the bolts on the variables, practiced the tricky parts, changed things that weren't working, and made better preparations. And most importantly, instead of digging into the feeling of failure, you were able to change your story about it. Instead of seeing failure as the inevitable outcome, you cast it as a one-time stumbling block on your path to something better.

What's Happening In the Aftermath of a Poor Performance or Launch

In the moments, days, and weeks after you bombed—the failed opening where no one showed, the terrible performance, the post that snowballed into bad media coverage, the audition where you choked, the interview where you said something embarrassing—you have a choice about the story you tell yourself. How are you going to treat yourself in the aftermath? Because as much as we want to believe that our performances show us where we are in life, it's how we deal with the performance afterwards that shows us where really are and where we're headed.

Reclaiming Your Power

We often go home bummed after a bad performance, but the more we replay it in our heads, the more we'll start making decisions about ourselves based on it. Sometimes we let it grow bigger than it needs to. Instead of letting it be something that happened that can help inform us for the next time, we take it as some kind of concrete truth about ourselves. We attach ourselves to it, and this can create a frozen feeling. We're afraid to move forward because we're afraid of repeating a situation like that again.

Be wary of this. Be diligent about noticing it and putting a stop to it. And remember this:

"Between stimulus and response there is space. In that space is our power to choose our response. In our response lies our growth and our freedom."

– Viktor E. Frankl, neurologist, psychologist, and Holocaust survivor

One performance does not determine who you are.

Before you allow yourself to begin building a fake idea of yourself around this one moment or performance, take the time to figure out why it didn't work and imagine doing something different before you give up. Create a story that this "failure" is actually helpful in your growth as an artist. Tell the new story that:

Good Performances Make You Want to Continue But Bad Ones Make You Better

Whether you've bombed a show or been totally on fire, it doesn't matter one way or the other. The success is in staying on the surfboard and riding the wave as best you can, no matter how rough the waters. When you're able to do this on stage, then it gets easier in life. The bumpy airplane can make you more adventurous if you let it, or it can make you more nervous when you fly. It's your choice—and it all depends on how you want to tell the story.

The Rebel wants to pretend they don't care if you have a bad performance, but in reality, they're the part of you that's mortified. Their flippant sighs of, "*I don't care! Whatever!*" are them trying to protect you by guarding you from hurt and disappointment. The Outlaw will use it as an excuse to ride further away on their horse away from everyone and everything. The Fabulist is in total denial— "*What? What performance?*" because the truth is too painful. But these times are when the Fabulist must be drawn in, sequestered to use their story-telling talent to spin your experience with some love and compassion.

An Artist's Indemnification:

You Are a Creature Made for Reaching

When you reach for something really high,

you don't always meet your goal but you can be left

with the sense of satisfaction for having reached,

and stretched yourself into a bigger shape.

But this other thing can happen where you let

yourself feel like a failure.

You feel like because you didn't meet the benchmark

that you set for yourself then you may as well

have not tried at all. You become nostalgic for your past

successes, forgetting all the while that

at the time of that success . . .

you were actually reaching even higher!

You've forgotten that the success that you're nostalgic for now

felt like a failure at the time.

You're hungry for a ghost of a happier self

that never even existed.

You could try to stop reaching.

You could let your arms hang at your sides.

You could be sad and complacent . . .

until one day you're reaching for something

in the back seat of your car and you pull a muscle

and you realize your job in life is not to shrink.

It is to continue reaching.

It is to be limber enough to reach without pulling your muscles

and without measuring yourself with a yardstick

because you are a creature made for reaching.

Eagles don't ask if they're higher now than they were yesterday

but they just enjoy the flight.

Alchemizing Your Pain Into Gain: Honing Your Artistic Voice

The great thing about being an artist is that we get to funnel our shadow side, our gremlins, our fears, our inner critical voices into our work. We get to use every bit of who we are in our work should we choose to. We have the freedom to alchemize the pain into something golden. When you see a successful artist with a clear artistic voice, it's because they've refined their message. They've honed in on who they are and the story that they're telling. They've found a way to take the stories they've been told (which harden into your 'inner critic') and use them in the stories they are telling (which become your artistic work).

Here are some examples of artists who have done this. Starting with comedians (who are the artists most often performing a heightened version of themselves on stage) I've taken a crack at identifying the stories they seem to be telling the world and then I took the liberty to imagine the stories they might have been told.

Stories They Are Telling	Stories They Might Have Been Told
Amy Schumer: The Anti-Lady	
"Women are human—we can be raunchy, sexual, smart, and vain all at the same time."	"Don't be so crass! Be a lady!"

If you look inside the jokes and the movies Amy Schumer has made, you can see that she's taken on the pressure that women feel to be always pretty, always together, always a lady. As a result, her sense of humor embraces the human side of female experience and presents a picture of herself that is sexual, flawed, crass, and therefore less flat and more holistic.

Dave Chapelle: The Fearless Truth-Sayer

"Everything is so f*ed up. . . But I'm doing okay."	*"Who do you think you are? Think you're something special?"*

Everything about Dave Chapelle's work these days tends to say, "Why yes, I do in fact think I'm pretty special at what I do." As he said in a recent special, "I'm so good at telling jokes, I start with a punchline and work backwards to get there just for fun." He acknowledges the opportunities he's been given as an artist and the crazy circumstances he's had to navigate, and he cracks open the door at these mysteries with the humorous gravitas of a war veteran telling tales that always end with some version of, "but I survived."

Adam Sandler: Adolescent Boy in Grown Man's Body

"I still find this funny. Isn't this fun? I don't care if you don't like it."	*"Eww, you're gross. You're so weird."*

Look at the slapstick and somewhat juvenile jokes in his movies, and you'll see that Adam Sandler has leaned into his flair for an adolescent sense of humor and made his career by addressing things that are gross and weird.

Ellen: Seeing The World Through Child-Like Perspective

"I'll take you at your word."	*"Grow up! Take this seriously!"*

Ellen tends to find the funny in taking what people say literally and riffing off that. She seems to (or pretends to) see the world through a child's eyes by questioning the obvious. Whereas at some point, I'm sure that had to be annoying for those around her: I can imagine them exasperated, "Ugh! You know what I mean! Be serious now!" She has made an entire career out of playing with literal translation.

Wanda Sykes: The Outsider In Her Own Home

"It's Not Normal!"	*"You're not normal! You're so strange!"*

Wanda Sykes' voice is so crystal clear. In her latest Netflix special, It's Not Normal, she talks about everything that's not normal, starting with the president of the United States and moving on to the oddity of her personal life circumstances (having a white wife and white kids). Even though she shares details of her life that are unusual, she does it in a way that we can all relate to. I would guess that she was always a little special and heard things like, "You're not normal," and now has learned to capitalize on that fact and tell unique stories that no one else could tell.

Iliza Schlesinger: The Girl Logic Analyst

"Women are great! But we're crazy! But we're powerful! But we're crazy!	*"You crazy bitch! You're so manipulative."*

Iliza Schlesinger has her finger on the pulse on what women are really like. She sees through the outward presentation and into the psychological depths of our actions (and our sometimes competing motivations). Her voice is so clear that even the title of her book emphasizes, Girl Logic: The Genius and The Absurdity. I wonder if she didn't hear some brandishing of "crazy bitch!" and now has made a career out of analyzing what that really means.

Other Examples:

Dancer, Maria Kochetkova: The Quirky Nymph

International prima ballerina Maria Kochetkova was told at the beginning of her career that she was "too short to stay" but she has made a career of her size, her quirky personality, and her seemingly endless passion and energy for dance.

"Your voice is your super-power."
  - Lisa Congdon

"Painting is self-discovery. Every good artist paints what he is."
  - Jackson Pollock

Rapper, Cardi B: The No Filter Hustler

Known for her inspirational success story as a stripper that re-invested her earnings into a music career, Cardi B was probably at some point told she was "too much"—or told to "tone it down" or "don't say that!" She has gone on to create a social media following of millions and an entire career by saying what she truly thinks.

Actor, Octavia Spencer: Self-Made Heroine

It's been reported that Octavia Spencer grew up hearing the story of Madam C. J. Walker, the African American hair-care entrepreneur whose story is told in the movie, Self Made, in which Spencer stars. From the roles that she plays to the movies she produces, you can see a career that builds on the very same stories of struggle and success that Spencer heard as a child.

Just like the artists above, you too have been told stories (through criticisms, admonishments, praise, or careless remarks) that have shaped you. Also just like the artists above you too have the freedom to use stories to inform the stories you tell through your art. It's just another part of your Love and Fear Elixir. Once you have some control over your own narrative and where it's taking you, not only does your own life and energy free up, but also the way you tell your stories through your art improves. And you can do it consciously.

What Are You Invoking? Questions to Hone Your Artistic Voice

Below are some questions to help you dig deep and not only understand your "inner critic" but also discover where it has been informing your work all along.

Part I. Your Own Gremlins

- What are some of the things you find yourself saying to yourself on a regular basis when you're in a mood to beat yourself up?
- What are the areas in your life where you feel insecure or shy?
- What are you terrified of doing?
- Where in your life have you embraced your strangeness, differences, faults, or difficulties?

Part II. Your Creative Output

- List all of the creative things you've done throughout your life.
- Are there similarities in the stories that you tell?
- What about the mood, style, or even the tactical approach (i.e., how you get down to creating)?
- What is the general perspective that you base your work on? (i.e., the world is good, the world is falling apart, etc.)
- What are you passionate about?
- What do you absolutely love?
- What can't you stand?
- Look for themes in your work: is there a story/stories that you find yourself telling again and again?
- What kind of response do you want to provoke from you audience?
- Do you have certain characters that you use again and again?

- Are there certain mythologies or fairy tales that can be linked to the narrative arc of your work?

- If your work isn't narrative, then how is it shaped by human activity, relationships, etc.?

- Is there always a certain outcome to your stories?

- Where do you like to begin a story?

- Where do you typically end? Before we know the resolution? Do you peek into the afterlife of the characters?

Part III. Your Artistic Heroes

- Name 5-10 of your favorite artists.

- What do you think is the story that they're telling on stage?

- What are similar things that they seem to say over and over again?

- What might you assume about their own gremlins based on their story?

Part IV. You and Them

- What do you love about these artists?

- What of these traits might you have in common with them?

- Where do you see an aspiring version of yourself in them?

What If You Were Just Honest?

After all of this talk about crafting your story, I want to circle back to the idea of vulnerability. It's important when crafting your story that you don't take it too far and try to change yourself until you're unrecognizable. The real beauty of what you have to offer as a performer lies in the truth of what you are and what has made you that way. That old Love & Fear Elixir again. If offering yourself up to connect with the audience is an antidote to fear, then your honesty or your authenticity is what you're offering up. When we connect honestly, we give something over that is worthy of attention. We surrender to being seen—really seen— and that is riveting. That is something to behold.

Unfortunately, baring your truths isn't always the easiest thing to do, especially when you're feeling worried, self-conscious, triggered, or not totally aligned with what you're doing on stage. As a performance coach who has worked with actors, composers, musicians and dancers, I know how destructive the fear of being vulnerable can be for an artist. Because what is performance without risk and vulnerability? It is mediocrity. Polite applause. Going over every detail endlessly while you eat cold saffron rice out of a tupperware container in bed afterwards, followed by a slow death of your passion over the next few years. Ouch.

What if it's easier than you think?

But what if... What if that kind of vulnerability, being totally open, isn't as hard as you think it is? What if it's easy? Maybe what's tough is partial honesty, half-vulnerability, the mediocrity of dipping your toe onstage but not revealing yourself fully.

Maybe that's the painful part.

These were the thoughts I found myself having after interviewing one of the guests on the Performers & Creators Lab Podcast, comedian Billy Procida. Procida hosts The Manwhore Podcast, where every week he talks to women he's hooked up with about sex, dating, sexuality, love—and why they didn't work out. Can you think of anything more vulnerable than that? I really can't. Billy found me through a call out for guests that I posted on a Facebook group, and after listening to his podcast, I was intrigued. How on earth could someone do that for four years and not be changed by it. How could someone share himself so vulnerably?

He says of being vulnerable on his show: People ask me, "How do you put that out there?" And I'm just like, "I don't know how I don't! Because unless I'm going to be an expert then why the hell else would you listen to me?"

He's recognized what is appealing to his audience and he understands that anything less doesn't make any sense. "I'm putting it all out there. That's what makes me different. I'm not a sex educator or a self-proclaimed dating expert. I do not pretend to be any of those things. So then why listen to me? Because I'm being vulnerable."

For Billy Procida, vulnerability has become the device he uses for the majority of his creative work. He has made a name for himself by focusing less on crafting something to share with you, laboring over the details beforehand, and more on the riveting quality of in-the-moment honesty. What really struck me after interviewing him is his fearlessness about being exactly what he is. While there are some things he keeps private, he is transparent with everything that he chooses to share. And while he does continue to hone his craft with every story he tells, and his hours and years of stand-up comedy experience, his vulnerability stays consistent. He may say it better, but he's still saying it with the same openness.

But sometimes people really don't like it.

Why You're Scared of Being Honest

It's not all fun, this job of letting it all hang out. Over the years, Billy has received backlash from listeners, including being called things like, "Bitch boy feminist pet." He walks a line between sex positivity and comedy, and those two worlds don't always mesh. He has had to deal with the public and social media hating, commenting, stalking. He told me that over the years, he's learning how to not get sucked into unnecessary drama and keep himself more centered.

There's nothing more riveting than honesty, and sometimes nothing harder than honesty. What if people see what's there and they don't like it? Performing artists are some of the most vulnerable people in the world.

The cost of honesty is that people might not like it and then ... does that mean they don't like us? Getting up and being honest in front of people is like saying:

Here's exactly where you can make fun of me or ... you can choose to connect with me.

I dare you to connect.

Sometimes they connect, they lean in, they respond favorably. Other times they take you up on the other dare with their faces, their silence, their boredom, or their disinterest. And then it's your work to recover and to say, "Oh well, so what!" And in the words of Brené Brown, you shout to the rooftops, "Even though I failed, at least I dared greatly!"

On the other hand, the prize is . . . maybe they do like it.

And then we experience being witnessed for all we are—flaws and all—yet still loved. Once you get a taste of it, you can't help but chase it.

The Pain of Halfway Honesty

I know what you're probably thinking, "So, Holly, are you telling me that in order to overcome my fear of being seen, I need to share more?" Well, sort of. I'm saying that the pain of being seen isn't about those parts that are seen, but rather it's about the effort of keeping concealed those parts of us that we're struggling to hide. Because vulnerability doesn't work in timid doses and that's where we often fail or fall short. That's when we come off as "trying too hard," "being too performative," or "missing the mark." We share something cringeworthy without the container of honest emotion to deliver it.

> "Who has time to make up stories when the truth is so much more interesting?"
> - Cecily von Ziegesar

When it comes to honesty and vulnerability, a lot of us hedge our bets: "How open do I need to be, really? Exactly how much does it take?" We reveal a corner, an elbow, a tale, feeling like we've put it all out there to later realize that we only put the scraps on the lawn and left the good stuff hidden inside. But the world is littered with half-truths. We're dying for something real.

So what about you, dear light-seeker and light-shiner: What do you reveal? And what do you hide? We often hide those things we deem unacceptable, unworthy, and we hold parts of ourselves in a secret shame. This can become our personal hell, our own internal dark cellar.

My grandmother had a cellar. She lived on a farm in Illinois, and she would occasionally ask me to go down to the cellar to grab a jar of this or that. But I didn't like doing it. It was dark down there, and there were cobwebs, and I couldn't imagine that there could be anything good to eat down there. But there was. We'd bring up jars of pickles or preserves, and lo and behold, they were delicious. Just an abundance of things there in the dark, waiting for the winter when they were needed. I think that in some ways, this is our winter. This is the time when we need things to come out of the dark. So what are you hiding? What have you squirreled away, or stored in the dark, afraid to open it? Afraid of what's grown there? What bits are you ready to reveal today? You may be surprised to find that they are delicious.

> "Truth is funnier than most things you can make up."
> - Margo Kaufman

A New Story Emerges

Here's the beautiful and final thing I must share with you about crafting your story: it comes naturally.

When you connect and then create out of that connection, the change to your story is inevitable.

Nothing ever stands still. Change is the only constant.

Movement, change, different paths are always opening up and calling us as long as we let them.

And what safer way is there to craft story than by being in connection and creativity?

With all the fun of crafting story, and with all of the tools I've shared here in this section, you can get lost in the details if you're not careful. So please remember that there is nothing here to overthink. The important thing is to stay plugged in and present in what's happening, and eventually the story will unfold.

Or in the words of Mary Poppins: "I shall stay until the wind changes."

Stay until the wind changes, dear artist, and trust you will know where to fly to next.

"Change is inevitable. Growth is optional."

- John C. Maxwell

Part IV

Things to Avoid:
Traps, Pitfalls, and Signs You're Heading in the Wrong Direction

Thinking You Have to Be Positive or Productive All the Time

Underlying Fears at Play: the Unknown, Not Enough

A calm person in the middle of madness knows when to put down the oars. Holding it together all of the time will make you harden and decrease your endurance and flexibility. Think of how you work out your muscles: You don't do leg days and arm days on different days for nothing. Just as your physical muscles need an opportunity to relax, so too do your creative productivity muscles.

> If you are constantly putting on a brave face, it becomes just that—something that you are "putting on" and faking instead of living from a real place of alignment.

Putting constant pressure on yourself to be "on" and productive mostly stems from the fear of the unknown. What's happening tomorrow? Will I be able to finish this then? Is time running out? I'd better force myself to get through this so I'll be prepared . . .

It's OK to slow down, to take your foot off the pedal, to not feel 100% great all the time. It's OK to disconnect, to stand still, to disallow, to feel the despair, the heartache, the grief of losing what you were looking forward to. To do anything less would be disingenuous. Feeling your feelings is an act of self-care, and it's a mistake to think you have to be making art in the middle of madness all the time. It's a little insane, really.

You can have bitchy moments.

Telling yourself otherwise is just one more act of perfectionism, one more critical voice you are heaping on your already burdened and weary shoulders.

Creating art should be the escape, the call, the inspired action. Not the duty. When it starts to feel like a heavy weight, just put it down for a while. You're allowed.

Your Love & Fear Elixir: Where do you push yourself too hard? When do you do it? Do you have tendencies during certain periods, or is it triggered by certain situations? What are the voices in your head saying to you when you force yourself to work harder than is healthy for you? Whose voices are they (e.g., your parents, your teacher, etc.)? What's a loving voice you can counter with? How do you like to spend your down time? What inspires you to relax?

Playing It Small

Underlying Fear: the Other, not Enough

I remember being at a friend's performance, and at the very end she publicly announced that I was in the audience and invited me up to dance on stage. I politely declined the offer, stayed seated, and immediately felt my spirit sink with disappointment. It was an awful feeling that hit me in my solar plexus as I asked myself:

Why did I commit my life to being an artist if I wasn't going to seize opportunities like this? Why was I playing it small?

This was years and years ago. I'm pretty good at jumping on any chance to be seen nowadays, but to this day, that memory and ones like it make me wince. And one thing I've learned from spending a lifetime on stage, in film, on TV (and inserting myself into people's news feeds and email boxes) is this:

As someone in the public eye, you have to be willing to take up space.

You must be willing to take up more space than most allow themselves. It's just plain crazy to note how many artists, entrepreneurs, and speakers—professional or not, successful or not—sometimes shrink from being BOLD, announcing themselves, displaying themselves, mounting their work, inserting themselves, blasting themselves, promoting their shows or content.

You might say you find it "tacky," but what's really going on is something altogether different.

There are two things you have to decide in order to feel in alignment with putting yourself out there and taking up space with your art:

1. You have to believe that there is infinite room for everyone who wants to be there.

This is where the fear of not enough comes into play. I think sometimes we get sold on the idea that it's a zero sum game, that there is only so much pie to go around and that if you take up space, then it's taking it away from someone else. In order to feel fully aligned with being visible, you have to believe that there is room for everyone. Audiences will find what they like, and it's not up to you to decide "how much is too much."

2. You have to believe that you're worth it.

When you take up space—with your art, your performance, your content—you are sending a powerful signal that says, "I matter." You are declaring to the world that what you're saying or expressing through this medium is something worth seeing. And that means you gotta feel worthy of it.

Now, if you're nodding your head in agreement as you read this, and you've checked these off the list, and you're STILL feeling queasy at the idea of taking up space, then it could very well be that you are simply not used to being visible. Taking up space requires that willingness to sit in some tense moments. Maybe you were trained somewhere along the way to break that tension for survival or for the comfort and convenience of others. So, you may find that you're simply uncomfortable with taking up space because it's unfamiliar.

8 Ways You Can Train Yourself to Take Up More Space and Be Visible

Culturally, we are conditioned to play it small, keep ourselves in line, be polite, don't overshare. The list goes on and on. Many of us have been conditioned this way again and again "Don't talk so loud!" "You're too much!" "What an attention whore!" And so on and so forth. We've been conditioned out of our desire to be bold and big and visible. You may have already discovered this throughout this book as you've reflected on your past experiences.

Here are eight easy things you can start doing today to train yourself to take up more space:

1. Stretch Yourself Out When You Sit Or Stand

Try this: Next time you're in a group, try sitting back in your chair, spreading your arms out around you (I've been so bold as to drape them over the chair of the person next to me if I know them), or propping them up behind your head. Instead of squishing your legs together or crossing them, try placing them apart on the floor.

2. Take Up Two Seats On Public Transit

Ok, so clearly if it's a packed bus or someone needs a seat, you'll give it over. But practice this when there are a few seats available. Sit in-between the two seats taking up two seats.

3. Insert Yourself Into Conversations Without Waiting for the Person to Finish

Yes, this is technically interrupting. "And," the voice in your head says, "isn't that rude?" Well, we are taught that it's rude, and yet powerful people do it all the time. Here's the trick to doing it artfully: Dovetail the conversation. That means that you meet the conversation where it is, snatch up the tail of the moment, and take the conversation where you'd like it to go.

Try this: Jump in as someone is finishing a point by repeating the last few words they said, then saying, "I hear you and . . . " then insert your point of view.

4. Take Up An Extra Chair With Your Backpack or Your Purse

Next time you're at a restaurant, ask them for a chair to place your purse on. This was taught to me by a friend of mine who believes it is bad luck to put a purse on the floor (not to mention dirty). I find that while not always practical and not always convenient, it can stretch you to be more comfortable taking up space.

5. Play Chicken with Oncoming Pedestrians

Here's a fun one: When you're walking on a sidewalk with other foot traffic, see if you can not move out of the way to oncoming pedestrians. Instead of yielding, allow others to move around you. What's interesting about this is that in the beginning you will find that people may bump into you, but with practice and confidence, you begin to create a greater sense of space around you such that most oncoming people will feel compelled to move around you. It's almost like your aura extends and gets bigger alongside your confidence.

> *(Now, obviously, be careful doing this in the case of bikes or people who aren't paying attention or moving very quickly. Don't put yourself in a position to get hurt!)*

6. Practice Spaces of Silence with Your Close Friends

When your friend asks you a question, turn to look at them slowly, pause . . . and see how long you can wait before answering them. Make a little game of it. Notice when your friends are pulled in and intrigued by this, or when you hold too long and the rubber band snaps and they become disinterested or turn away.

7. Walk Into Your Next Audition (or On Stage) More Slowly

All right, so you can't be a total diva about it, I get it. But I've been in casting waiting rooms before and I've watched what happens when an actor's name is called. They lean forward and jump up quickly, sending a signal to their body that they're in a rush. This can send you into a tailspin of anxiety. Instead, gather yourself and stand as though you are in the comfort of your home. Decide to get up and go into the kitchen for a snack. Gently, relaxed, and confident. You will feel the difference, and—BONUS!—you send off signals of confidence by doing this.

8. Wait Before You Begin

If you ever have the chance to watch a lineup of performers (for example, at an audition, a showcase, or in stand-up comedy), watch how the most riveting performers begin with a little silence—just standing there, taking in the room and letting the room take them in. This is Step 1 of the Watermill Exercise, and a good habit to get into. Look around the room and notice your surroundings, then take a deep breath for three seconds. It gives people a moment to focus their attention on you. The room comes to you—and it signals to yourself and to your audience that you are worthy of taking up space.

When "Outside In" Practices Don't Help

These practices I suggest above are all an "outside in" approach, meaning that you are taking outward action in order to try to retrain or change something within yourself. I know this sort of "outside in" approach doesn't work for everyone. If you try these things above and find they aren't helping the deeper issues that you have with taking up space, then it might be time to get some support or take an intensive to help you unlock the real reason you play small or feel uncomfortable being visible. Some things you can learn and utilize from books, and some things take deeper work. In this case, I suggest you seriously consider getting some one-on-one support from a professional coach or therapist that you vibe with.

Your Mission, Should You Choose to Accept It: Pick one of these suggestions above and commit to it for a week. How does it feel? Stick with it until you feel less uncomfortable about it. Persist through some of the discomfort. See if you can find a place in yourself that relishes this new space you're taking. See if you can connect with the pleasure in it.

Hogging the Stage

Underlying Fear: not Enough, the Other

On the flip side of playing it small is being a stage hog, otherwise known as "stealing the show."

People always talk about stealing the show like it's a good thing, but when I think of it, I think of upstaging. It's something that most performers will run into from time to time. Now, hogging the stage or upstaging is different from being a star, playing to your highest potential, or shining fully—all of those are good things that can inspire others on stage with you to rise to a higher standard so you all win. That is good stuff. What I'm talking about is someone who switches the rules on you and leaves you trying to catch up.

Being a stage hog fuels the belief that there is not enough (in this case, time, attention, adoration) and gives into the concern, if not fear, of the other. You aren't trusting that you'll have your time in the spotlight, and you aren't trusting the people you work with to give it to you, so you simply take it. This creates a crack in the trust you share and leads to disconnection, which snowballs into even more fear. And it robs people of the opportunity to share with you.

Think of the hero who doesn't let anyone else step in, even if someone else could do it better. It doesn't serve anyone to think you have all the answers or that you are the only one worth seeing. It's a foolish waste of resources. Whether we're talking about producing a show or dealing with a crisis, more voices, more diversity, and more opinions can create a better final product.

How to Hold Your Own When You Perform with a Stage Hog (and How Not to Be One)

No matter what kind of show you're doing, there is always a set of rules that makes the whole thing work—and you know someone has upstaged you when they step outside of the rules to get a little of theirs. It's shameless. So, what do you do when that happens? Our tendency is to shrink. To freeze up. Of course it's best to go with the flow, but sometimes they've sped ahead so fast that you don't know where to jump in.

There are two ways you can manage it in that moment. First, you could try to play along and keep up. Alternately, you can counterbalance them. Play cool to their hot or hot to their cool. Create a dialogue out of the imbalance. But really, I want to say:

"Just don't work with them again."

If you feel like you have a close enough relationship where you can point it out to them in hopes that they'll change, then try that first; but often times the person who will up stage you will do so again and again in different ways. Until they confront their own fears and learn how to work with others they are a like a loaded gun to you – you'll never know when they're going to go off. So, it makes sense to not work with these types of people, or do so as little as possible.

This advice may seem harsh, especially because all of us have likely been guilty of upstaging at some point. But I'm hoping we get it out of our system early and quickly. Most of us learns not to hog the stage early on because it just feels kind of off afterwards. You're left with the sense of over-reaching. As you're reading this are you feeling a little bit embarrassed about yourself for hogging the stage in the past?

Well, good - that means you're not a total narcissist, you're just human.

Art as Activism

It's always been my opinion that art by its very nature is activism. No matter what you're doing, whatever the theme, there is a point of view and you are promoting it, shedding light on it, creating empathy around it, or creating conversation about it by ACTIVELY doing something about it. Presenting art is activism.

When it comes to activism, we each have to use our platform as we so choose as we so see fit. You can begin by asking yourself where you feel compelled to tell those stories that aren't being told. What stories do you feel haven't been reflected that will haunt you until you tell them? How can you make room for stories that aren't yours, but that you see as ones you'd love to hear about nonetheless?

For me, activism and art is all about sharing the stage. Being an activist doesn't mean that you can't shine, you can't raise your hand, you can't take opportunities. It doesn't mean you have to take a step back—it means encouraging others to rise with you. To be willing to look to your left and to your right, behind you and in front of you, and make the people around you look good.

Whether you are venturing out onto the stage or into the world, the bottom line for sharing the stage is the same:

Take people with you when you shine.

Your Love & Fear Elixir: When have you been a stage hog in the past? Be honest! Almost everyone has done this. How did it make you feel? What was the payoff? What did you expect to get from hogging the stage? How did it actually play out? When have you been on the other side of it and had someone do it to you? How did that make you feel? When do you feel at your best, as though you've truly shared the stage? Where in your life could you share the stage a little more than you do?

"When a man is denied the right to live the life he believes in, he has no choice but to become an outlaw."

– Nelson Mandela

Mishandling the Potent Stuff Made for Seeking

Underlying Fear: The Unknown

Art is a powerful substance. Which is why it can devour you. Think of rock stars that die from suicide or overdose by the time they're twenty-seven. The stars that get publicly humiliated and then go into hiding. Being in the public eye and yet keeping yourself sensitive and open enough to be at the epicenter of a powerful creative flow is an intense combination. You have to grow the psychological--and dare I say it, spiritual—muscles to endure this creative energy.

In my sophomore year of college, I went through a really tough time in my life: I was doing hallucinogens on a semi-regular basis, I had an agonizing relationship with my boyfriend, and I was starting to audition for my acting roles poorly. I was anxious all the time and feeling like my life was falling apart. At that time, a mentor of mine, Raphael—who sported a long white beard and called himself a 'wizard'— had been observing me going through this, and one day he said to me:

"Holly, are you doing hallucinogens for fun?"

Huh? Why, I wondered, what was I supposed to be doing with them?

I admitted I was doing them for fun, and he responded, "Oh no, no wonder you're falling apart. You can't do that for fun! That's a sacrament. That's potent stuff for seeking."

I tell this story because, in a lot of ways, I think art can be a substance like that. It makes you see things differently, and it can feel like a ride that's hard to jump off once you're on it. But if you approach it flippantly, it spits you out and makes you anxious about everything.

The potency of this energy is evidenced by the very existence of stage fright. The nervousness, shakiness, and nausea are all a result of the sheer power of what is running through you as you perform. Talk to just about any artist and at some point they will shy away from taking all the credit for their work. Oh, they might credit their teachers or other artists, but really? They are at a loss to understand this genius any more than you. They are trying to give words and appraisal to the higher creative genius that comes through.

> Art is potent stuff. Handle with care.

They shirk the praise because at some point or another they've had the lightning bolt hit them. They've had the "creative downloads" that come into their minds, fully formed and perfect. Not always, but they've had them. They've had them and they're addicted. They love the rush. Oh, don't get me wrong! A lot of us experience some struggle at some point, the hard labor of sticking with a creative product and seeing it through to its end. We experience the highs and lows, but we'd do it all over again for those few glorious times where we got the rush - for those white water rafting rides down the river of creative flow.

We hook up, plug in, and surrender ourselves to this powerful energy—and we need to take extra care not to burn out or burn ourselves up because of this. . . Not everyone wants to do this. Not everyone is willing. And yet the world needs it. Craves it. And will happily use us for it.

From the Sacred to the Profane

The actor Rainn Wilson said, "The making of art is no different than prayer." Art evolved out of shamanism. It was the shaman, or the healer that played the drum, that told the story, that invoked the mysterious and otherworldly. Have we forgotten our place and our role as artists? Have we lost touch with the art of leading others into the dark and then ushering them back into the light? When we compete with each other for a gig, struggle financially, argue with our families to go to art school, berate ourselves in our own minds, do we forget that this thing we want to do is sacred?

Have we forgotten that art is potent stuff for seeking?

Art turned into mere entertainment, and we forgot what was happening to us. We experience its power, but we don't always honor it. We pay for that incredible rock and roll concert, but we don't think too deeply about how we'll be changed by it.

> Over time, art has moved from the sacred to the profane.

It has gone from an experience that we shared in and respected and even held as reverent to one that we commodified and objectified. We package it, sell it, stream it, and trade it like bitcoin to the far reaches of the world.

Do we try to return to something long ago? To the way things were? I don't think so. It's not my opinion to ever try to "get back" but rather to build upon where we are. We have to ask ourselves, how can we use the infrastructure, the technology, and the momentum of what's been built in order to be empowered shamanic artists within it? Instead of mourning the past, we have to build upon it and put ourselves, not in opposition to it, but on the leading the wave of its momentum.

It's a sacrament. It's commanding stuff for seeking. It makes you see things differently and it can feel like a ride that's hard to jump off once you're on it. But if you approach it flippantly, it spits you out and makes you anxious about everything.

Part V

Your Potential Impact

Turning Fear Into Light

Humans have a narrow range where we live most of the time. We only allow ourselves to experience slivers—or tips of the iceberg—when it comes to emotion. Distaste, jealousy, hope, darkness, depression, despair, rage, ecstatic joy—these things leak out in different ways when we have no place to express them. Artists do this emotional labor on our behalf. Remember at the beginning of this book when I told you that when you step on stage, you're assuming the role of the center of attention? You have the responsibility to do something with that attention. Excite them. Make them feel something! Transport your audience into another world!

There is not a lack of happiness in the world, but rather a deficiency of attention toward it. When you focus your attention toward your happiness—toward connection, toward your presence, toward your new story—you turn everyone else's attention toward it as well. Isn't that a neat trick?

The Ecstatic Transmission

I was nineteen when I had my first full-bodied orgasmic and ecstatic experience on stage...

Insert sound effect of "screeching to a halt." Now, you may be thinking, "What am I reading?" But it's not what you think. Or should I say, it's much more than you think. That experience was more than just an orgasm. It was an ecstatic opening. And it was the key, the beginning of so much more I had to unravel in this body and lifetime. It was the beginning of every discovery I've made ever since.

Here's what happened:

Before the performance, the drummer and I had worked out a drum solo in the middle of the piece, but for some reason when we got to that part in the performance, instead of playing what we had rehearsed, he played something else entirely... and with the crack of his drum, it was like a lightning bolt shot through my body. In that moment of the unexpected, I knew that I had a choice: I could either choke and freeze up, or I could ride the wave of this new thing unfolding.

"Many of my favorite shamans are rock stars. They probably don't even know they're shamans, but they know how to get to ecstasy and back and how to take others with them. They may not have a license, but they know how to drive."

– Gabrielle Roth

I chose to ride that wave, and when I did, I felt the waves of pleasure that rolled throughout my body. My face was hot and flushed with rapture, and I felt like my arms extended to the back of the room, like my whole being reached out to the edges of the universe.

It was intensely pleasurable, pure, ecstatic, a full-body orgasm like I'd never experienced before.

And in that moment, I did something that was significant for not only myself, but for the audience as well: I took what was a potentially scary and choking experience (being thrown out of what we'd rehearsed) and I made the choice, albeit unconsciously fast, to go with what was happening instead of fighting it. I connected with what the drummer was doing, stayed present to the moment, and created a new story.

I turned fear into light.

I've gone on to have other similar experiences in my life, and I've begun to recognize not just the personal gains but the potential power in transmitting these kinds of choices and experiences to the audiences who are watching them.

Think about it: as a performing artist, you are meant to transfix, to entrance, to captivate people. And once you do, you have the ability to transmit to them whatever's happening inside you. And if you are turning fear into light, then you are teaching every. Single. Person. Just by watching you and synching up with your experience to do exactly that.

Your potential impact is infinite.

"Everywhere we go, we're looking for the sun. Nowhere to grow old, we're always on the run. They say we'll rot in hell but I don't think we will. They've branded us enough, outlaws of love."

– Adam Lambert

Joining the
Army of Artists

What if ... by reading this book I could empower you to create work that helped the world evolve emotionally? To spread empathy through new stories? To weave new ideas into the very fabric of our lives? To reconnect everyone on the planet with their inner power and innate creativity? And what if we were able to do this together? To create a sort of army of artists dispatched to the far corners of the world, turning fear into light.

The impact of this could be enormous. It is my belief that even one creative mind, opened to its own genius, has the power to change the world.

I hope that by reading this book you've worked through your personal fears and anxiety so that you can go out into the world and make art, no matter the madness going on around you. But the macrocosmic potential of doing that, of leading by example, is that through your art you can transmit that ability to do just that. You become the light in the darkness.

When you resonate with your creativity,
you resonate with all creativity everywhere.

When you reach for something new,
you reach for all that's new.

When you imagine something different,
you imagine differences that work together.

When you push the boundaries of what seems possible, you
find the cracks in what seemed impossible.

Every Artist Is
A Hypnotist

You are crazy powerful.

Do you know how powerful you are?

You have the power to change someone's emotional state, the power to build empathy, the power to bridge worlds by telling a story, the power to change people's minds by showing them something they've never seen before.

One YouTube video can reach millions. One viral song, speech, or social media post... Your reach is infinite.

You know who already knows this? You know who wields this power and cashes in on it?

Advertisers.

Marketing experts who make content to lure you in and sell you stuff.

They are the unabashedly "shameless" creatives of today, willing to take up space and demand your attention. They buy information about where you hang out, learn about what you're interested in, and then insert themselves into wherever that is.

They are willing to take up space, and they're doing a good job of it.

And how are they doing it? Fear.

They spend their creative powers making sure we feel afraid of missing out, making a fool of ourselves, or not measuring up.

And so, we must trade one trance for another. Theirs rides on fear, but yours, oh! Yours is so much better!

So, you there! You creative, wily chaos creator! Rebel! Fabulist! Outlaw Maker! Hear me when I say that you too have the power to have that kind of impact. Consider these final words your call to duty to join the army of artists around the world who are consciously and continually creating. I implore you to use the tools in this book to move through your blocks, to create, and consider what it is you're offering. Where are you taking us? What is the spell you're putting us all under?

The requirement to making art in the middle of madness

Is your unflinching claim to this space.

The art is what you decide to do in that space.

The healing is where you decide to take them.

And so now, all you have to do is begin. . .

An Artist's Invocation for Beginning

Today I will begin in the dark.

I will begin anywhere.

I will carve my creation from my self-doubt,

Look to the things I don't know how to say,

And become soft inside the hard lines.

I will make friends

with the old characters from my fairytales.

Trot out their plot lines

Exhaust all the options.

I'm just letting you know:

I'm beginning.
Right here.
In the dark.

And you're here too.

Acknowledgments

There are so many wonderful teachers, friends and mentors who have the sowed seeds of wisdom in my life from which this book sprang forth. I'd like to thank Jesse Koren and Sharla Jacobs for amplifying the importance of connection which they teach in their work with speakers, holistic coaches and entrepreneurs. Like seeing a shape take form out of an inkblot, their teachings on connection enabled me to articulate so much of what has become important in my work with performing artists. I'd also like to thank cartoonist and storyboard artist, Mike Kunkel. The chapter entitled, "Seeing Your Life Like A Storyboard Artist" was a direct result of taking a storyboarding class with him at Animation Mentor and hearing his breakdown of different shots that a storyboard artist uses.

I'd also like to thank my "COVID wives": Bernadette LaNoue, Hannah Watson, Laura Hanks, and Sarah Burke – I could not have stayed so grounded and sane during this pandemic without you. And a huge thank you to my son who has had to struggle through his last years of high school and applying to colleges throughout the writing of this book while also enduring a pandemic. It's not easy to be quarantined alone with just your mom for a year, and you know what, kid? All things considered, I think we did pretty good. . . and also, thank you for punching up my jokes.

Finally, I'd like to acknowledge all of the women and female identifying people throughout history whose voices have been muted, who have been persecuted, burned, shamed and excommunicated: the brave women and persons, the outspoken ones, the witches, the courtesans, the sacred prostitutes and the single moms. This book is for them as well as for the temple dancers, the devadasis, and the chorus girls. All the wisdom in this book: connection, vulnerability, how to build tension and break it, how to be present in the moment, weave a new story – how to turn fear into ecstasy – these are in many ways ancient teachings passed down from them. This wisdom has been suppressed and buried, but it has survived in whispers, stories shared in small circles, and through the journey of many artists. And so, it has made its way through me and onto these pages. From these women who've been kept in the shadows the keys to our survival on this planet come forth. The divine feminine is waking up and speaking through all of us. Won't you listen and speak her name?

About the Author

Holly Shaw is a performance coach, creativity researcher and hypnotherapist whose first book, The Creative Formula, became an Amazon bestseller shortly after it was published in 2016. She has spent a lifetime on stage, television and film as an actor, dancer, and now stand-up comedian and over the years has facilitated and directed many workshops and productions including teaching at the SAG/AFTRA conservatory in both Los Angeles and San Francisco. Her podcast, Performers and Creators Lab, was named One of The Most Outstanding Podcasts of 2019 by Databird Research.

Through all of her offerings Shaw has helped thousands of creatives, some of them Grammy nominated and Emmy Award winning artists, Hollywood actors, and internationally renowned dancers, in order to help them overcome stage fright, anxiety, and blocks so that they can create the work they were born to make and become undeniably magnetic performers without feeling like they're selling out or losing their sanity. Currently, she produces a live, COVID compliant comedy show, The Comedy Edge, in Oakland, California where she lives with her son. Follow her life in realtime on Instagram @hollyshawspritely where she shares regular updates or visit PerformersandCreatiorsLab.com to get free resources and learn more.

Influential Books and Additional Resources

Aldridge, David and Jorg Fachner. *Music and Altered States: Consciousness, Transcendence, Therapy and Addictions.* London: Jessica Kingsley Publishers, 2006.

Brenman, Margaret and Merton Gil, M.D. *Hypnosis and Related States: Psychoanalytic Studies in Regression.* International Universities Press, Inc. 1961

Brown, Brené. *Rising Strong: How The Ability To Reset Transforms The Way We Live, Love, Parent, and Lead.* New York: Penguin Random House LLC, 2015.

Hagen, Uta. *A Challenge for the Actor.* New York: Scribner, 1991.

Hart, Mickey. *Drumming At the Edge of Magic: A Journey Into The Spirit of Percussion.* New York: HarperCollinsPublishers, 1990.

Hill, Napoleon. *Think and Grow Rich.* New York: The Random House Publishing Group, 1937.

Mellon, Nancy. *Storytelling & The Art of Imagination.* Cambridge, MA: Yellow Moon Press, 1992.

Nhat Hahn, Thich. *Being Peace.* Berkeley, CA: Parallax Press, 1987.

Robbins, Tom. *Even Cowgirls Get The Blues.* New York: Bantam Books, 1976.

Ronson, Jon. *So You've Been Publicly Shamed.* New York: Riverhead Books, 2015.

Roth, Gabrielle. *Maps to Ecstasy: A Healing Journey for the Untamed Spirit.* Novato, CA: Nataraj Publishing, 1989.

Shlesinger, Iliza. *Girl Logic: The Genius and The Absurdity.* New York: Hachette Books, 2017

Steiner, Claude. *The Original Warm Fuzzy Tale.* Austin, TX: PRO-ED, Inc., 1977.

Made in the USA
Las Vegas, NV
16 December 2020